EAT
YOURSELF
HAPPY

EAT YOURSELF HAPPY

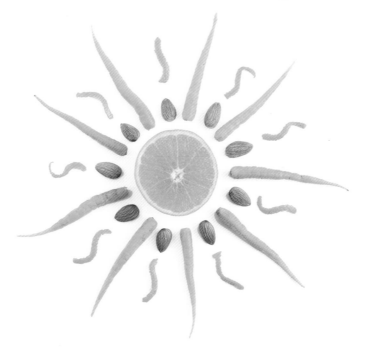

INGREDIENTS & RECIPES
FOR A GOOD MOOD, EVERY DAY

GILL PAUL

NUTRITIONIST: KAREN SULLIVAN, ASET, VTCT, BSC

hamlyn

An Hachette UK Company
www.hachette.co.uk

First published in Great Britain in 2014 by Hamlyn,
a division of Octopus Publishing Group Ltd
Endeavour House
189 Shaftesbury Avenue
London WC2H 8JY
www.octopusbooks.co.uk

Editor: Jo Wilson
Art Director: Jonathan Christie
**Photographic Art Direction, Prop Styling
and Design:** Isabel de Cordova
Photography: Will Heap
Food Styling: Joy Skipper
Picture Library Manager: Jen Veall
Assistant Production Manager: Caroline Alberti

ISBN 978-0-600-62748-7

A CIP catalogue record for this book
is available from the British Library

Printed and bound in China

10 9 8 7 6 5 4 3 2 1

All reasonable care has been taken in the
preparation of this book but the information
it contains is not intended to take the place of
treatment by a qualified medical practitioner.

People with known nut allergies should avoid
recipes containing nuts or nut derivatives,
and vulnerable people should avoid dishes
containing raw or lightly cooked eggs.

Both metric and imperial measurements have been
given in all recipes. Use one set of measurements
only, and not a mixture of both.

Standard level spoon and cup measurements
are used in all recipes
1 tablespoon = 15 ml spoon
1 teaspoon = 5 ml spoon

Ovens should be preheated to the specified
temperature – if using a fan-assisted oven,
follow the manufacturer's instructions for adjusting
the time and temperature. Large eggs should be
used unless otherwise stated.

Some of the recipes in this book have previously
appeared in other titles published by Hamlyn.

CONTENTS

INTRODUCTION

We all feel down now from time to time; it's the natural response to sad news, such as redundancy, relationship breakdown or serious illness affecting us or someone we love. However, some people are more prone to depression than others: they get down more often and then have trouble shifting their mood back onto an even keel. For a minority, the depression is so severe they require medical help, such as drugs or therapy, just to get through the week.

When we are down we tend to opt for the wrong kinds of foods, choosing sugary foods for a quick burst of energy and alcoholic drinks to dull the pain, yet these things make depression worse. There are dozens of different types of depression, with different causes, but almost all are improved by eating the right kinds of foods to synthesize ample supplies of brain neurotransmitters, address vitamin and mineral deficiencies and stabilize blood sugar levels. No matter how low you feel, wise food choices will make you feel happier – and the benefits will start straightaway.

What makes us feel low?

There are a number of factors that affect mood. Genetics play a part; you are more likely to suffer from depression if one of your parents was depressed. Difficult childhood experiences, such as sexual abuse, bullying or the loss of a parent or sibling, can also make you more prone to depression when you are older. And certain personality types get depressed more often than others – for example, those with low self-esteem. But scientists are also aware that our biochemistry plays a major role in affecting our moods.

MRI (magnetic resonance imaging) scans made of the brains of people suffering from depression indicate that there may be deficiencies of certain neurotransmitters (the chemicals responsible for passing on signals). Hormonal imbalances can also trigger depression, which is why some women get depressed and anxious when their oestrogen levels drop before periods or during the menopause. Lack of sunlight is an additional factor that can make us depressed because sunshine stimulates oestrogen, serotonin and the synthesis of vitamin D.

How to eat yourself happy

1. Eat enough protein

Some key amino acids, the building blocks of proteins, must be included in our diets because we can't manufacture them ourselves. For example, the amino acid tryptophan is required to make serotonin, the neurotransmitter that controls mood, sleep patterns and appetite. Likewise phenylalanine is essential for the production of noradrenaline and adrenaline, which affect energy levels, and dopamine, which regulates the emotions. Eating a wide range of good-quality proteins, and including protein in at least two meals or snacks a day, will help to ensure that you produce enough of these all-important mood-balancing neurotransmitters.

2. Top up the B vitamins

Those with low levels of B vitamins (especially B6, B12 and folate) are at greater risk of depression, because these substances are required to keep the nervous system healthy and control the production and balance of neurotransmitters. Eating plenty of bananas, avocados, chicken, wholegrains and leafy green vegetables will help to replenish your stores.

3. Feast on fish

Those who eat a lot of fish are less prone to depression than those who don't. It's because the omega-3 oils found in fish, particularly one called EPA, help to build brain cell connections and receptor sites for neurotransmitters. The more EPA in your blood, the more serotonin you will make – and the happier you'll be.

4. Choose the right carbs

The types of carbohydrates we eat affect our mood and behaviour. Avoid refined carbohydrates, such as white bread, white pasta, white rice and all processed foods, and cut down on your sugar intake to even out blood sugar levels, prevent dips in energy and mood swings. Don't be tempted to avoid carbs altogether, though, because they are necessary for many crucial processes in the body,

including the manufacture of serotonin. Opt for unprocessed carbs with plenty of fibre that will be absorbed more slowly into the digestive system and have less of an effect on blood sugar. That means eating plenty of wholegrains, brown rice, pulses and vegetables.

5. Look after your gut

It's long been known that stress and anxiety can cause problems in the digestive tract, but recent research has suggested that it also works the other way round and gut problems can be responsible for triggering depression. Combat this by eating foods that encourage healthy digestion, such as plenty of fibre and live yogurt to replenish bacteria in the gut. You should aim to drink lots of water every day, too.

6. Dose up with vitamin D

Vitamin D deficiency can also trigger depression. We get vitamin D through the food we eat and through exposure to sunlight on our skin. Optimize your chances of beating depression by eating plenty of vitamin-D-rich foods (such as oily fish and eggs) and getting out into daylight as much as you can.

7. Keep clear of caffeine and alcohol

Caffeine drinks (coffee, tea and colas) stimulate the release of insulin, which mops up sugar in the blood, causing lowered levels of sugar and giving you an energy dip. Stick to one or two cups of coffee a day when you're feeling down. And alcohol is a depressant which will make it harder to come out of a depression.

Getting started

When you are feeling low, you may experience a loss of appetite and tend to skip meals – or, conversely, you may over-eat, looking for comfort in food. Looking after yourself physically is the first step to curing the blues. Make sure you eat small regular meals and snacks, which will improve symptoms rapidly by keeping your blood sugar levels stable. This should stop you having cravings for sweet or fatty foods.

....

Follow the meal planner on pages 30–33 for a powerful mood booster. If you would like to address specific symptoms, such as stress, irritability, loss of libido or sleep problems, check the problem solver on pages 26–29 for key foods you should be eating. Pages 12–25 list the foods and their benefits, and give suggestions as to how to incorporate them in your diet.

There are other easy ways you can make a difference. Exercise may help psychologically by boosting your self-esteem, and it is also thought to have a biochemical effect as it causes the release of endorphins, which block pain receptor sites in the brain. Talking to other people, whether it is your doctor, a trained counsellor or a trusted friend, is also highly beneficial. The main thing is not to struggle on alone. If you have been depressed most of the time for more than two weeks and it is affecting your ability to live a normal life, or if you have had any suicidal thoughts, ask your doctor for help. That is what he or she is there for.

....

Even if your depression is not primarily caused by biochemical imbalances but is the result of genetics or life events, you should still find that eating the right foods helps. It's an all-round healthy way of eating, it's delicious – and you deserve it.

....

HAPPY
SUPERFOODS

SUPERFOODS

These powerhouse foods help to relieve symptoms of depression and anxiety, and will boost your health on all levels.

Turkey

✔ Elevates mood
✔ Reduces anxiety
✔ Balances blood sugar levels
✔ Encourages a healthy nervous system
✔ Promotes healthy sleep

Turkey is one of the most important foods in a depression-busting diet, and its high levels of tryptophan do everything from encouraging restful sleep to boosting immunity. It is low in carbohydrates and fat, and high in protein.

It's rich in...

→ Tryptophan, an amino acid which stimulates the production of the feel-good chemical serotonin and encourages restful sleep
→ Zinc, to help balance blood sugar levels and boost your immune system
→ Choline, which protects the nervous system
→ Selenium, which helps to balance moods and prevent anxiety and depression

Use in... a chef's salad, with Swiss cheese, mixed leaves, hard-boiled eggs and cherry tomatoes; in place of beef in a Bolognese sauce; as a sandwich filler, mixed with lemon mayonnaise and crunchy cucumber; in a stir-fry with Asian greens and soy sauce.

SEE: TURKEY & PEANUT NOODLE SALAD, P78;
CAULIFLOWER & TURKEY BIRIYANI, P96;
TURKEY, LENTIL & APRICOT STEW, P97;
THAI TURKEY BURGERS WITH KALE CRISPS, P98

Sunflower seeds

✔ Elevate mood
✔ Encourage nerve health
✔ Promote healthy sleep patterns
✔ Protect against damaging effects of stress
✔ Reduce anxiety

Sunflower seeds have long been considered a natural antidepressant, and the multitude of vitamins, minerals and other nutrients they contain make them a nutritious addition to a healthy diet and a great booster of energy and mood.

They are rich in...
→ Magnesium, to regulate nerve function and balance calcium levels, encouraging restful sleep
→ Tryptophan, to enhance the production of feel-good serotonin, thus lifting mood
→ Vitamin B6, to encourage the release of the body's natural depression-fighting chemicals
→ Manganese, a component in nerve health and required for thyroid hormone production, low levels of which can lower mood

Use in... trail mixes, with other seeds, nuts and dried fruit for snacks; cereals and muesli; salads and dips for extra flavour and crunch; crumble toppings; biscuits and muffins, for an extra boost of healthy fats; as a coating on fish, such as sea bass.

SEE: MUESLI WITH PEACHES & YOGURT, P38; APPLE & CRANBERRY GRANOLA, P42; BANANA SUNFLOWER SEED COOKIES, P62; CREAMY ROASTED PEPPERS WITH MIXED GRAINS, P105

Mackerel

✔ Improves mood
✔ Eases symptoms of depression
✔ Enhances energy levels
✔ Encourages relaxation
✔ Helps to treat symptoms of seasonal affective disorder (SAD)

A number of studies have found that mackerel has a significant antidepressant effect, working to boost energy levels while restoring feelings of calm and balance. Rich in healthy fats, it also plays a number of other roles in the body, encouraging good health on all levels.

It's rich in...
→ Omega-3 oils, which have been shown in several studies to relieve many symptoms of depression, including low mood, as well as to help regulate brain function
→ Vitamin D, to boost immunity and ensure calcium is balanced for healthy nerve function and natural mood lift, particularly in the darker winter months
→ Magnesium, to aid nerve function and promote relaxation and healthy sleep
→ Vitamins B3 and B12, which affect mood and other brain functions

Use in... Asian salads; in place of kippers in kedgeree; herby mackerel pâtés for healthy snacks and light meals; fish cakes with lemon and herbs; cook with a harissa glaze for a North African-style dish; barbecue with ginger and lime.

SEE: MACKEREL PATÉ ON RYE CRISPS, P52; MACKEREL & ASPARAGUS TART, P86; MACKEREL FILLETS WITH OAT TOPPING, P90

Avocado

✔ Encourages healthy brain function
✔ Helps to balance hormones
✔ Improves energy
✔ Boosts immunity
✔ Balances blood sugar
✔ Improves concentration

An excellent source of healthy fats, avocado is full of mood-boosting nutrients which can work to lift your mood while ensuring optimum health on all levels. The balance of fats, protein and fibre helps to stabilize blood sugar levels, improving energy, stamina and concentration.

It's rich in...
→ Magnesium, to boost immunity and help promote relaxation and normal sleep patterns
→ Fibre, to balance blood sugar levels and promote healthy appetite and digestion
→ Vitamin B6, which encourages healthy iron levels in the body, thus improving energy levels, while also helping to keep the brain functioning optimally
→ Healthy proteins, to boost alertness and performance

Use in... sandwiches instead of mayonnaise; guacamole; add to salads; spread on toast instead of butter; make an avocado dressing to top a salad; blend with vanilla extract, live yogurt and honey for a creamy, nutritious smoothie.

SEE: SMOKED SALMON & AVOCADO CORNETS, P56; MISO BROTH WITH PRAWNS, P72; SALAD NIÇOISE WITH ARTICHOKES & ASPARAGUS, P80; WARM RAINBOW SALAD, P84

Dark chocolate

✔ Reduces stress levels
✔ Lifts mood
✔ Improves alertness
✔ Encourages relaxation
✔ Raises serotonin levels
✔ Reduces pain and symptoms of stress

Dark chocolate is rich in a variety of nutrients and chemicals that work directly on the neurotransmitters in your brain, to boost mood, alertness and relaxation, while reducing pain and many of the symptoms of stress. Countless studies point to its ability to encourage a sense of wellbeing, and this is one ingredient that should be on the menu of anyone hoping to become happier.

It's rich in...
→ Flavonoids and other nutrients that have been shown to reduce stress hormones in the bloodstream
→ Phenylethylamine, which causes changes in blood pressure and blood sugar levels, leading to increased alertness and excitement
→ Theobromine, which enhances physical and mental relaxation
→ Chemicals that prompt the release of endorphins, the body's pain-relieving and pleasure-promoting hormones, and serotonin, the antidepressant hormone

Use in... spicy chillies and curries, for a deeper flavour; melt and blend with a banana and live yogurt for a rich, nutritious smoothie; grate over morning porridge for an instant pick-me-up; add a handful of dark chocolate chips to baked goods; melt over fruit and nuts for a nourishing snack.

SEE: ICED BERRIES WITH DARK CHOCOLATE SAUCE, P112; DARK CHOCOLATE & RASPBERRY SOUFFLÉ, P114; CHOCOLATE-DIPPED FRUIT, P124

Live yogurt

✔ Reduces stress hormones
✔ Helps ease anxiety and depression
✔ Encourages healthy digestion
✔ Boosts immunity
✔ Promotes relaxation
✔ Improves energy levels

A recent study found that the probiotics (healthy bacteria) contained in live yogurt may alter brain chemistry and can help in the treatment of anxiety and depression-related disorders. What's more, it helps to lower stress hormones in the bloodstream.

It's rich in...

→ Calcium, which can encourage a healthy nervous system as well as restful sleep
→ Probiotics, which improve immunity and ease symptoms of depression and anxiety
→ Iodine, which boosts the production of thyroid hormones to encourage healthy energy levels and metabolism
→ Vitamin B12, which is required for the production of oxygen-carrying red blood cells and the health of the nervous system

Use in... breakfast cereals and muesli instead of milk; as a base for fruit smoothies, to slow down the transit of fruit sugars in the blood; on sandwiches instead of mayonnaise; mix with lemon rind and herbs as a salad dressing; blend with a little vanilla sugar as an accompaniment for crumbles, cakes and other baked goods.

SEE: MUESLI WITH PEACHES & YOGURT, P38; BANANA OAT SMOOTHIE, P39; NUTTY PASSION FRUIT YOGURT, P40; APPLE & CRANBERRY GRANOLA P42; BRAZIL NUT & BANANA PARFAIT, P110; ICED BERRIES WITH DARK CHOCOLATE SAUCE, P112; FIG & GRAPE TARTS, P120

Oats

✔ Nourish the nervous system
✔ Ease anxiety
✔ Balance blood sugar levels
✔ Encourage calm
✔ Boost libido
✔ Enhance memory and energy levels

Oats are renowned for their ability to encourage the health of the nervous system, and have long been considered a 'nervine' tonic. They are rich in fibre and slow-release carbohydrates which can help to balance blood sugar levels and stabilize mood. Oats also contain healthy fatty acids to promote overall wellbeing.

They are rich in...

→ Slow-release carbohydrates, they are associated with the production of the mood-enhancing neurotransmitter serotonin
→ B vitamins, to encourage the health of the nervous system
→ Soluble and insoluble fibre, to improve digestive health and the absorption of nutrients from food, and to balance blood sugar
→ Zinc, which is required for healthy immunity, libido, hormone balance, energy levels and memory

Use in... homemade muesli and baked breakfast goods; as a topping for crumbles and sweet and savoury pies; as a coating for baked fish or chicken; in homemade soda bread.

SEE: MUESLI WITH PEACHES & YOGURT, P38; BANANA OAT SMOOTHIE, P39; APPLE & CRANBERRY GRANOLA, P42; FIG & APRICOT FLAPJACKS, P58; MACKEREL FILLETS WITH OAT TOPPING, P90; BRAZIL NUT & BANANA PARFAIT, P110

Bananas

✔ Lift mood
✔ Encourage calm
✔ Raise serotonin levels
✔ Boost energy
✔ Enhance digestion
✔ Aid restful sleep
✔ Increase alertness

Bananas are one of the most nutritious fruits. The high levels of potassium nourish the nervous system, while helping to ensure a good supply of oxygenated blood to the brain. High levels of vitamin B6 make bananas ideal for treating menstrual-related depression.

They are rich in...

→ Tryptophan, which encourages the production of serotonin, raising mood, facilitating relaxation and deep, restful sleep
→ Potassium, which boosts alertness and concentration, and lifts mood
→ Vitamin B6, to aid the production of norepinephrine, a neurotransmitter which stimulates brain activity and enhances alertness and concentration, while helping to produce serotonin
→ Fibre, to encourage blood sugar balance and aid digestion

Use in... crêpes or add to American-style pancakes for a nutritious breakfast; keep a few bananas in the freezer and add to live yogurt, honey or fresh fruit for an instant iced smoothie; bake alongside pork instead of apples; bake with brown sugar or honey for a warm dessert.

SEE: BANANA OAT SMOOTHIE, P39; STRAWBERRY
& BANANA MUFFINS, P59; BANANA SUNFLOWER
SEED COOKIES, P62; BRAZIL NUT & BANANA
PARFAIT, P110

Strawberries

✔ Balance moods
✔ Aid concentration
✔ Encourage digestion
✔ Help ease symptoms of premenstrual syndrome (PMS) and SAD
✔ Boost vitality and virility
✔ Raise energy levels

Like all berries, strawberries are rich in antioxidants which have a host of beneficial effects on overall health and wellbeing, including boosting energy levels and protecting the brain from the effects of stress. Their high fibre levels promote efficient digestion and absorption of nutrients. As an excellent source of vitamin C, they improve immunity, too.

They are rich in...
→ Manganese, for a healthy nervous system and energy production
→ Anthocyanins, powerful antioxidants which improve health on all levels and protect against many different degenerative diseases
→ Phenols, which have anti-inflammatory benefits to ease aches and pains
→ B vitamins, to encourage a healthy nervous system and balanced moods

Use in... smoothies; sprinkle on breakfast cereal and muesli; freeze and dip in dark chocolate sauce for a frosty, delicious treat; add to muffins, sweet breads and other baked goods for moisture and added nutrients; purée and set with a little gelatine for a nutritious fruit jelly; add to green salads with goats' cheese and toasted walnuts.

SEE: STRAWBERRY, WATERMELON & MINT
SMOOTHIE, P36; STRAWBERRY & BANANA
MUFFINS, P59; ICED BERRIES WITH DARK
CHOCOLATE SAUCE, P112

Kale

✔ Boosts immunity
✔ Encourages brain health
✔ Enhances digestion
✔ Raises energy levels
✔ Stimulates detoxification and liver health, thus balancing hormones

Kale contains more than 13 times the daily recommended intake of vitamin K, a nutrient required for a healthy nervous system and brain function. A host of antioxidants provide support for your immune system and act as anti-inflammatories, easing aches and pains.

It's rich in...
→ Iron, to encourage the production of red blood cells, which carry oxygen in the blood
→ Vitamin C, to boost immunity, to help prevent damage to cells as a result of stress, and encourage a healthy metabolism
→ Calcium, potassium and vitamin A, essential for a healthy nervous system
→ Manganese, for energy production

Use in... salads with a little red onion, red peppers and sultanas; braise with apples and top with walnuts and a sprinkling of cinnamon; stir into soups, stews and casseroles; steam and top with lemon rind, sea salt and olive oil; add to wholegrain pasta with a light pesto and a good grating of Parmesan cheese.

SEE: MINTED KALE SOUP, P68; THAI TURKEY
BURGERS WITH KALE CRISPS, P98

Brazil nuts

✔ Balance hormones
✔ Improve energy levels
✔ Ease mood swings and lift mood
✔ Reduce anxiety

High in healthy monounsaturated fats, brazil nuts contain extremely high levels of selenium, a mineral known for its anti-anxiety, mood-lifting properties. Just three brazil nuts each day have been shown to increase levels of this nutrient significantly, affecting emotional health.

They are rich in...

→ Selenium, which helps to balance mood and prevent anxiety and depression
→ Zinc, which is required for hormone balance, energy levels and memory
→ Magnesium, to aid restful sleep and promote healthy relaxation
→ B vitamins, required for metabolism and to eliminate symptoms of depression, fatigue and nervous disorders

Use in... salads with feta cheese, grapes and mixed salad leaves; dip into dark chocolate for a mood-lifting snack; chop and add to muffins, chocolate brownies, cookies and sweet breads; make a pesto with ground brazil nuts, lemon juice and rind, fresh tarragon, olive oil and Parmesan cheese.

SEE: NUTTY PASSION FRUIT YOGURT, P40;
APPLE & CRANBERRY GRANOLA, P42;
BRAZIL NUT & BANANA PARFAIT, P110

Peanuts

✔ Balance blood sugar
✔ Encourage serotonin production
✔ Promote restful sleep
✔ Boost memory
✔ Help symptoms of PMS and post-natal depression
✔ Help prevent over-eating

Peanuts are a great source of healthy monounsaturated fats, as well as vitamin E, niacin, folic acid and good-quality protein. They are as rich in antioxidants as many fruits and, with a low-GI rating, can help to balance blood sugar levels.

They are rich in...

→ Vitamin B3, which promotes normal brain functioning and boosts memory power
→ Tryptophan, which is essential for the production of serotonin, a key element in mood regulation and healthy sleep
→ Folic acid, to encourage a healthy nervous system
→ Manganese, which can help reduce symptoms of PMS and post-natal depression, while regulating neurotransmitters norepinephrine and serotonin

Use in... salads with crunchy fresh vegetables; add to Asian curries, stir-fries and noodle salads; spread peanut butter on wholegrain breakfast toast or oatcakes, or just eat a spoonful of peanut butter as a mid-afternoon snack; try peanut butter and banana sandwiches, a North American staple.

SEE: TURKEY & PEANUT NOODLE SALAD, P78;
CHICKEN & PEANUT STEW WITH BROWN RICE, P94

Eggs

- ✔ Regulate mood
- ✔ Encourage concentration and alertness
- ✔ Support the adrenal glands, which release stress hormones
- ✔ Boost energy levels
- ✔ Stabilize blood sugar
- ✔ Promote the release of serotonin

Eggs are a rich source of healthy proteins, which not only balance blood sugar and stabilize appetite, but also provide a wealth of amino acids to lift mood and help to facilitate restful sleep. They're particularly useful for symptoms associated with stress.

They are rich in...

→ Tryptophan, to encourage the release of the brain neurotransmitter serotonin, which lifts mood and helps to establish healthy sleep patterns
→ Choline, necessary for a healthy brain and nervous system, improving both memory and mood
→ Selenium, the antidepressant mineral which also helps to boost immunity and balance mood
→ Iodine, which encourages the health of the thyroid gland, responsible for energy levels and metabolism

Use in... herby omelettes with spinach and mushrooms; try eggs scrambled with chives and topped with smoked haddock; eat hard-boiled eggs stuffed with live yogurt, chives and dill for a filling, healthy snack; chop and add to salads; scramble and serve in a wholewheat tortilla with fresh salsa, guacamole and black beans.

SEE: BAKED EGGS WITH SPINACH, P43; POTATO & SWEETCORN HASH WITH FRAZZLED EGGS, P46

Sesame seeds

- ✔ Antidepressant effect
- ✔ Balance blood sugar
- ✔ Regulate hormone production
- ✔ Encourage production of serotonin
- ✔ Reduce anxiety
- ✔ Reduce symptoms of PMS

Sesame seeds are incredibly rich in calcium and magnesium, both of which help to promote a healthy nervous system, relaxation and restful sleep. They lower glucose levels in the blood, thus balancing blood sugar, and provide a dose of tryptophan, to help sleep and mood.

They are rich in...

→ Sesamol, a chemical found to have antidepressant effects in cases of chronic stress
→ Vitamin B6, to help combat symptoms of PMS, support the nervous system and encourage relaxation
→ Zinc, which helps to prevent damage caused by stress
→ Vitamin B1, which has calming properties and aids nerve function

Use in... Asian salads; any type of hummus, including chickpea, butter bean and edamame (soya) varieties; use sesame oil in stir-fries and salad dressings; add to cookies, flapjacks and other baked goods for mood-boosting snacks; try the darker-coloured seeds (black, brown and red) to add flavour to curries and other Indian dishes.

SEE: SESAME SNAPS, P55; FIG & APRICOT FLAPJACKS, P58; SESAME-CRUSTED SALMON, P88; ORANGE, GINGER & SESAME RICE PUDDING, P122

Wholewheat

✔ Promotes healthy digestion
✔ Balances blood sugar levels
✔ Promotes the release of serotonin
✔ Reduces symptoms of PMS
  and post-natal depression
✔ Encourages a balanced weight

Rich in tryptophan, which encourages the release of serotonin, and an excellent source of healthy fibre and a little protein, wholewheat is an excellent addition to a mood-boosting diet. It has high levels of B vitamins which support the nervous system, and also contains antioxidants to protect the body from stress-related damage.

It's rich in...
→ Complex carbohydrates, which balance blood sugar and lift mood, aiding the production of serotonin
→ Manganese, to help reduce symptoms of PMS and post-natal depression, while regulating the neurotransmitters norepinephrine and serotonin
→ Fibre, to balance blood sugar levels, promote healthy digestion and encourage healthy absorption of nutrients from food
→ Betaine, which reduces inflammation and associated aches and pains

Use in... wholewheat pastas with light vegetable sauces; try wheatberries (available from health food shops) in place of quinoa or rice in filling salads; sprinkle grains over soups, stews and casseroles; serve wholegrain tortillas or pittas with hummus or peanut butter.

SEE: WHITE BEAN HUMMUS WITH PITTA BITES, P50; THAI TURKEY BURGERS WITH KALE CRISPS, P98; PENNE WITH TOMATO, ARTICHOKE & OLIVE SAUCE, P104

Garlic

✔ Boosts immunity
✔ Helps produce serotonin
✔ Lifts mood
✔ Supports the nervous system
✔ Encourages digestion and
  reduces bloating
✔ Increases energy levels
✔ Reduces fatigue
✔ Eases anxiety
✔ Promotes wellbeing

A recent German study found that raw garlic not only elevated the mood of the study participants, but also reduced fatigue, anxiety and irritability. Garlic has also been used in the treatment of addictions, and is great for boosting the immune system.

It's rich in...
→ Vitamin B6, which encourages healthy iron levels, improving energy levels and maintaining optimal brain function.
→ Manganese, for a healthy nervous system
→ Selenium, vitamin C and calcium, all of which have antidepressant effects and promote relaxation and wellbeing
→ Tryptophan, which is the amino acid responsible for promoting restful sleep and the production of the neurotransmitter serotonin

Use in... anything! Crush raw cloves and add to salad dressings, stews, dips, casseroles and soups; roast and spread on wholegrain bread; use to flavour curries and pasta sauces; crush, add to a little mayonnaise flavoured with the juice and rind of one lemon; stuff inside poultry when roasting, and mash into the gravy.

SEE: ROASTED GARLIC CROSTINI, P54; TURKEY SOUP WITH LEMON & BARLEY, P69; SQUASH, CHICKPEA & SWEET POTATO TAGINE, P106

Asparagus

- ✔ Balances blood sugar
- ✔ Reduces irritability
- ✔ Increases libido
- ✔ Encourages healthy digestion
- ✔ Supports the nervous system
- ✔ Increases energy levels
- ✔ Improves immunity

Asparagus is one of the richest sources of rutin (a natural substance found in plants) which, together with vitamin C, can help to protect the body from infections by stimulating the immune system. It also contains a chemical which balances insulin levels, evening out blood sugar levels and, through that, mood swings and irritability.

It's rich in...

- → Vitamin K, which is required for a healthy nervous system and brain function
- → Folic acid, to reduce inflammation and support the nervous system
- → Prebiotics, which encourage the growth of immune-busting, digestion-enhancing probiotics in the gut
- → B vitamins, to encourage the health of the nervous system, promote healthy metabolism and energy levels, and balance blood sugar levels

Use in... salads; stir into risottos and primavera pasta sauces; steam and serve with a little lemon and sea salt; roast with lemon rind and olive oil; steam and wrap with prosciutto or smoked salmon for a quick snack; sauté with tofu or chicken; steam and add to omelettes with wild mushrooms or goats' cheese.

SEE: SALAD NIÇOISE WITH ARTICHOKES & ASPARAGUS, P80; GINGER SCALLOPS WITH ASPARAGUS, P85

Watermelon

- ✔ Boosts immunity
- ✔ Eases headaches and irritability
- ✔ Relaxes blood vessels
- ✔ Reduces fatigue
- ✔ Encourages healthy sleep patterns
- ✔ Encourages alertness

The flesh, rind and seeds of this delicious, juicy fruit can be eaten to provide a wealth of key vitamins and minerals which support health on all levels. It was traditionally used to lift depression and to balance hormones, and its high antioxidant content encourages immunity.

It's rich in...
- → Water and natural electrolytes, to rehydrate, ease headaches, reduce irritability and increase energy levels
- → Calcium, to nourish the nervous system and promote restful sleep
- → Vitamins B1 and B6, to balance hormones and encourage nerve transmission throughout the body
- → Potassium, for brain health and increased alertness

Use in... salads, topped with feta cheese and toasted pecans; blend in smoothies with a little live yogurt and a few sprigs of mint; purée with kiwi, mint, orange rind and yellow melon and serve as a refreshing cold soup.

SEE: STRAWBERRY, WATERMELON & MINT SMOOTHIE, P36; WATERMELON, GINGER & LIME GRANITA, P108; TROPICAL FRUIT SALAD WITH GREEN TEA SYRUP, P121

Ginger

✔ Stimulates digestion
✔ Eases nausea
✔ Reduces muscle pain and headaches
✔ Lifts mood
✔ Encourages a sense of calm
✔ Stimulates the taste buds
✔ Regulates blood sugar levels

In traditional Chinese medicine, ginger has been used for centuries in the treatment of depression and other emotional problems. Various studies performed in the last few years have verified the fact that it is calming and, in some cases, mimics the action of antidepressants. Its warming qualities also make it useful for aches and pains.

It's rich in...
→ The amino acid phenylalanine, which reduces pain, controls appetite, encourages alertness and improves memory
→ Threonine, an amino acid which boosts immunity and minimizes inflammation
→ Tryptophan, to encourage restful sleep and stable moods
→ Gingerol, an anti-inflammatory agent which eases nausea, promotes healthy digestion and eases pain

Use in... lemon and ginger tea, first thing in the morning to stimulate digestion; grate into curries, soups, stews and casseroles; use in Asian salads and stir-fries; stew with rhubarb for a delicious compote; stir into chocolate dishes and baked goods for extra flavour.

SEE: GINGER SCALLOPS WITH ASPARAGUS, P85; CHICKEN & PEANUT STEW WITH BROWN RICE, P94; CAULIFLOWER & TURKEY BIRYANI, P96; TURKEY, LENTIL & APRICOT STEW, P97; THAI BEEF & MIXED PEPPER STIR-FRY, P100

Figs

✔ Encourage brain and nervous system health
✔ Balance blood sugar
✔ Boost libido
✔ Enhance immunity
✔ Reduce inflammation and pain
✔ Balance hormones
✔ Improve liver health

Figs are an excellent source of vitamins, minerals and trace elements, encouraging health on all levels, as well as controlling blood pressure, easing muscular aches and encouraging healthy brain function.

They are rich in...
→ Omega-3 and omega-6 oils, to prevent inflammation and related pain, build muscle and tissue and enhance normal brain function
→ Potassium, to regulate blood sugar levels, prevent cramping, boost immunity and encourage the health of the heart and nervous system
→ Amino acids, such as arginine, which encourage libido
→ Soluble and insoluble fibre, to encourage digestion, balance blood sugar and mop up toxins to improve liver health and through that, hormone balance

Use in... fruitcakes and pies; chop and add to breakfast cereals and muesli; roast and purée into a compote to serve with live yogurt; serve with creamy blue cheese and walnuts on a bed of lettuce for a filling salad; marinate in balsamic vinegar and lemon juice and serve with mozzarella balls and pecans.

SEE: FIG & APRICOT FLAPJACKS, P58; BAKED FIGS WITH MASCARPONE, P113; FIG, RASPBERRY & PROSCIUTTO SALAD, P74

Barley

✔ Balances blood sugar
✔ Encourages digestion
✔ Boosts energy levels
✔ Encourages balanced weight
✔ Reduces anxiety
✔ Helps prevent depression
✔ Lifts mood

Barley is one of the oldest cultivated grains and, as a wholegrain, is rich in fibre, selenium and B vitamins, all of which play a role in balancing mood. In fact, one cup of barley contains more than half of your daily selenium requirement. The manganese it contains helps to provide an overall sense of wellbeing.

It's rich in...
→ Tryptophan, an amino acid which stimulates the production of the feel-good chemical serotonin and encourages restful sleep
→ Copper, to promote the uptake of iron to boost energy levels
→ Beta-glucan, a chemical which balances blood sugar levels and improves the body's response to glucose
→ Selenium, which helps to balance moods and prevent anxiety and depression

Use in... risottos, pilafs and puddings instead of rice; barley water, with fresh lemon juice to stimulate digestion and encourage calm; bulk out soups, stews and casseroles with barley to add healthy proteins, slow-release carbs and flavour; stuff into peppers with onions, pine nuts and feta cheese.

SEE: TURKEY SOUP WITH LEMON & BARLEY, P69

Lentils

✔ Balance blood sugar
✔ Promote healthy digestion
✔ Ease anxiety
✔ Reduce symptoms of depression
✔ Encourage the release of serotonin
✔ Raise energy levels
✔ Aid restful sleep

Lentils are a supremely nutritious member of the pulse family, with excellent levels of fibre to control blood sugar and folic acid to support a healthy nervous system. A good source of protein, lentils contain numerous amino acids to encourage a sense of wellbeing and actively work to reduce symptoms of depression.

They are rich in...
→ Soluble fibre, to help stabilize blood sugar levels, while providing a steady source of energy
→ Iron, to produce haemoglobin, which is necessary for a good supply of oxygenated blood
→ Tryptophan in high quantities, to encourage the release of serotonin, which lifts mood and helps sleep
→ Magnesium, the 'anti-stress' mineral which decreases the release of the stress hormone cortisol

Use in... soups, stews, casseroles and curries; serve cool or warm as a salad, with goats' cheese and lemon juice; use instead of rice as a bed for fish, curries and tagines; use in dhal, a nutrient-rich Indian dish; braise with chilli and oranges.

SEE: LENTIL & PEA SOUP, P66; TURKEY, LENTIL & APRICOT STEW, P97

Artichokes

✔ Encourage digestion
✔ Improve health of the nervous system
✔ Enhance metabolism
✔ Help restore healthy brain function
✔ Boost immunity
✔ Reduce symptoms of stress
✔ Ease irritability
✔ Promote hormone balance

Antioxidant-rich artichokes are brimming with nutrients to help lift mood and keep the symptoms of depression at bay. A rich source of minerals such as copper, calcium, iron and potassium, they naturally boost energy levels while protecting the liver, thus encouraging hormonal balance.

They are rich in...

→ Vitamin K, for a healthy nervous system and brain function
→ Vitamin C, to help balance the stress hormone cortisol in the body, boost immunity and ease digestion
→ Inulin, a prebiotic which stimulates the growth of healthy bacteria in the gut, thereby aiding digestion and encouraging healthy elimination
→ Calcium, to ease anxiety and restore nervous system function

Use in... salads, with roasted vegetables; use jars of marinated artichokes in pasta sauces, antipasti plates and Mediterranean salads; in sandwiches, with basil, pesto and mozzarella cheese; steam and serve with lemon butter or lemon-infused yogurt; fry with mussels or use as a base for vegetable terrines.

SEE: SALAD NIÇOISE WITH ARTICHOKES
& ASPARAGUS, P80; HERBY ARTICHOKE
CASSEROLE, P102; PENNE WITH TOMATO,
ARTICHOKE & OLIVE SAUCE, P104

Grapes

✔ Lift mood
✔ Improve concentration
✔ Increase serotonin levels
✔ Enhance oxygen flow to the brain
✔ Boost immunity
✔ Encourage healthy digestion
✔ Reduce inflammation

Grapes are full of essential vitamins, minerals and trace elements. In particular, resveratrol, found in the seeds and skin of grapes, has been shown to increase blood flow to the brain, improve concentration and promote higher levels of antidepressant chemicals serotonin and noradrenaline.

They are rich in...

→ Manganese, a component in nerve health and required for thyroid hormone production, low levels of which can lower mood
→ Vitamin K, to improve brain function and promote a healthy nervous system
→ Fibre and slow-release carbs, for better blood sugar balance, better insulin regulation, and increased insulin sensitivity
→ Phytonutrients, such as flavonoids and resveratrol, to encourage healthy digestion and immunity, and aid concentration

Use in... salads, with feta cheese and almonds; use frozen, as a snack to keep blood sugar levels balanced; in fruit tarts; alongside berries and bananas in nourishing smoothies; braise with chicken and walnuts; serve in a creamy sauce with sole, for Sole Véronique.

SEE: BEETROOT, GRAPE & FETA SALAD, P79;
FIG & GRAPE TARTS, P120; TROPICAL FRUIT
SALAD WITH GREEN TEA SYRUP, P121

WHAT'S YOUR PROBLEM?

The functional foods on the following pages work to heal specific parts of your mind and body, targetting and relieving the symptoms of depression. Decide which symptoms affect you and choose from the foods and recipes that help combat them. These icons are used throughout the recipe section to highlight which recipes offer the most effective treatment.

Low mood

Brazil nuts, spinach, oranges, grapefruit, herring, brown rice, spelt, edamame beans (soya), kidney beans, crab, turkey, green tea, kale, apricots, almonds, blueberries, dark chocolate, grapes, asparagus, ginger, barley, garlic, mackerel, sesame seeds, bananas, sunflower seeds.
Recipes Include:
Mackerel pâté on rye crisps, p52; Orange, ginger & sesame rice pudding, p122

Addictions

Kale, cabbage, romaine lettuce, beetroot, carrots, berries, grapefruit, ginger, eggs, brazil nuts, turkey, dark chocolate, peppermint, mackerel, cod, chickpeas, rye, strawberries.
Recipes Include:
Potato & sweetcorn hash with frazzled eggs, p46; Rare beef & baby beetroot salad, p76; Warm rainbow salad, p84; Turkey, lentil & apricot stew, p97

Anxiety

Peaches, blueberries, almonds, oats, dark chocolate, salmon, broccoli, brown rice, kelp/seaweed, milk, turkey, melon, beef, peanuts, edamame beans (soya), grapefruit, cherries, romaine lettuce, barley, ginger, garlic, sesame seeds, brazil nuts.
Recipes Include:
Muesli with peaches & yogurt, p38; Broccoli & almond soup, p70; Tomato, tofu & hot pepper salad, p82

Irritability

Tuna, salmon, mackerel, oats, black beans, pumpkin seeds, artichokes, dark chocolate, spinach, bananas, peanuts, brown rice, cashews, cabbage, edamame beans (soya), cod, sunflower seeds, asparagus, figs, watermelon, garlic, brazil nuts.
Recipes Include:
Salad niçoise with artichokes & asparagus, p80; Herby artichoke casserole, p102

Fatigue	**Depression**	**PMS**	**Poor concentration**

Fatigue

Hazelnuts, live yogurt, sesame seeds, spinach, chickpeas, cocoa, pomegranate, figs, eggs, kale, beetroot, apricots, coconut, cranberries, dates olives, cinnamon, salmon, brazil nuts, blackcurrants, watermelon, asparagus, garlic, mackerel, lentils.
Recipes Include:
Nutty passion fruit yogurt, p40; Baked eggs with spinach, p43; Olive & sun-dried tomato scones, p64

Depression

Wholegrains, oats, nuts, seeds, pulses, brown rice, brewer's yeast (or Marmite), quinoa, cabbage, brazil nuts, dark chocolate, sweet potatoes, kiwi, peppers, oranges, carrots, melon, apricots, grapes, artichokes, barley, garlic, turkey, mackerel, lentils, sesame seeds, bananas, sunflower seeds, salmon.
Recipes Include:
Banana & sunflower seed cookies, p62; Chocolate-dipped fruit, p124

PMS

Sunflower seeds, dairy produce, bananas, oranges, wheatgerm, salmon, sesame seeds, black beans, live yogurt, mackerel, tomatoes, cranberries, barley, strawberries, tuna blueberries, oats, watermelon, kale, artichokes, spinach, brazil nuts.
Recipes Include:
Sesame snaps, p55; Minted kale soup, p68; Watermelon, ginger & lime granita, p108

Poor concentration

Dark chocolate, oranges, pecans, walnuts, rosemary, avocado, spelt, quinoa, popcorn, blueberries, eggs, dairy produce, spinach, squash, potatoes, mango, asparagus, strawberries, watermelon, grapes, artichokes, ginger.
Recipes Include:
Eggs Benedict with smoked salmon, p44; Smoked salmon & avocado cornets, p56; Fig & grape tarts, p120

Over-eating

Chicken, edamame beans (soya), eggs, chickpeas, black beans, lentils, rye, wholewheat, dark chocolate, walnuts, almonds, peanuts, live yogurt, salmon, popcorn, coconut, apple cider vinegar, figs.
Recipes Include: Roasted garlic crostini, p54; Chicken & peanut stew with brown rice, p94; Herby artichoke casserole, p102; Dark chocolate & raspberry soufflé, p114

Mood swings

Wholegrains, pulses, tuna, salmon, halibut, cheese, yogurt, green tea, dark chocolate, mushrooms, almonds, brazil nuts, pistachios, blueberries, pomegranate, cinnamon, leafy green vegetables, watermelon, ginger, barley, garlic.
Recipes Include: Blueberry & mint smoothie, p60; Turkey soup with lemon & barley, p69; Sesame-crusted salmon, p88

Aches & pains

Salmon, ginger, cherries, olive oil, green tea, walnuts, flaxseeds, edamame beans (soya), turmeric, grapes, sage, spelt, quinoa, rye, cocoa, brazil nuts, oats, apricots, avocado, bananas, broad beans, garlic, butternut squash, sweet potatoes.
Recipes Include: Stir-fried tofu with prawns & rice noodles, p91; Brazil nut & banana parfait, p110; Cherry & nectarine pavlova, p118

Winter blues

Salmon, mackerel, almonds, eggs, kale, sweet potatoes, brazil nuts, turkey, dark chocolate, oats, strawberries, avocado, Romaine lettuce, bananas, dairy produce, pineapple, sour cherries, barley, garlic, lentils, sesame seeds.
Recipes Include: Mackerel pâté on rye crisps, p52; Smoked salmon & avocado cornets, p56; Turkey soup with lemon & barley, p69; Brazil nut & banana parfait, p110

Lack of desire

Celery, shellfish, pineapple, bananas, avocado, almonds, mango, peaches, strawberries, eggs, figs, garlic, dark chocolate, cocoa, chilli peppers, honey, pumpkin seeds, asparagus.
Recipes Include: Courgette & Stilton fritters, p47; Fig & apricot flapjacks, p58; Miso broth with prawns, p72; Ginger scallops with asparagus, p85

Low self-esteem

Blueberries, carrots, butternut squash, tomatoes, kale, spinach, romaine lettuce, alfalfa, cherries, grapes, tuna, salmon, almonds, dates, rye, chickpeas, lentils, broccoli, mackerel.
Recipes Include: Butternut squash & ricotta frittata, p48; Broccoli & almond soup, p70; Beetroot, grape & feta salad, p79; Mackerel & asparagus tart, p86

Sleep problems

Turkey, bananas, potatoes, honey, oats, almonds, flaxseeds, sunflower seeds, cherries, tuna, peanuts, cheese, live yogurt, brown rice, lentils, quinoa, dates, mango, watermelon, ginger, barley, garlic, brazil nuts.
Recipes Include: Potato & sweetcorn hash with frazzled eggs, p46; Sesame snaps, p55; Goats' cheese, apple & broccoli salad, p73; Turkey & peanut noodle salad, p78

Post-pregnancy blues

Avocado, coconut, flaxseeds, apples, rye, wholewheat, oats, strawberries, pumpkin seeds, dairy produce, brown rice, sweet potatoes, lentils, dark chocolate, blueberries, eggs, brazil nuts, kidney beans, sesame seeds, watermelon, artichokes, sunflower seeds.
Recipes Include: Strawberry, watermelon & mint smoothie, p36; Lentil & pea soup, p66

PUTTING IT ALL TOGETHER

Meal Planner	Monday	Tuesday	Wednesday
Breakfast	Muesli with peaches & yogurt, p38	Baked eggs with spinach, p43	Apple & cranberry granola, p42
Morning snack	Chocolate-covered brazil nuts	½ avocado with 1 teaspoon lemon mayonnaise	Boiled egg
Lunch	Ginger scallops with asparagus, p85	Beetroot, grape & feta salad, p79	Tomato, tofu & hot pepper salad, p82
Afternoon snack	Sesame snaps, p55	Olive & sun-dried tomato scones, p64	Chocolate-dipped fruit, p124
Dinner	Cauliflower & turkey biriyani, p96	Squash, chickpea & sweet potato tagine, p106	Mackerel fillets with oat topping, p90
Dessert	Baked figs with mascarpone, p113	Dark chocolate & raspberry soufflé, p114	Watermelon, ginger & lime granita, p108

WEEK 1

Thursday	Friday	Saturday	Sunday
Pink grapefruit with maple syrup	Nutty passion fruit yogurt, p40	Courgette & Stilton fritters, p47	Eggs Benedict with smoked salmon, p44
Smoked salmon & avocado cornets, p56	Banana sunflower seed cookies, p62	Fig & apricot flapjacks, p58	Handful of almonds
Lentil & pea soup, p66	Fig, raspberry & prosciutto salad, p74	Salad niçoise with artichokes & asparagus, p80	Goats' cheese, apple & broccoli salad, p73
Strawberry & banana muffins, p59	Mackerel pâté on rye crisps, p52	Roasted garlic crostini, p54	White bean hummus with pitta bites, p50
Penne with tomato, artichoke & olive sauce, p104	Turkey, lentil & apricot stew, p97	Creamy roasted peppers with mixed grains, p105	Chicken & peanut stew with brown rice, p94
Cherry & nectarine pavlova, p118	Orange, ginger & sesame rice pudding, p122	Tipsy blueberry & mascarpone pots, p116	Iced berries with dark chocolate sauce, p112

Meal Planner	Monday	Tuesday	Wednesday
Breakfast	Apple & cranberry granola, p42	Nutty passion fruit yogurt, p40	Strawberry, watermelon & mint smoothie, p36
Morning snack	Blueberry & mint smoothie, p60	Mackerel pâté on rye crisps, p52	Handful of grapes & Brie
Lunch	Miso broth with prawns, p72	Warm rainbow salad, p84	Mackerel & asparagus tart, p86
Afternoon snack	Chocolate-covered brazil nuts	Banana sunflower seed cookies, p62	Roasted garlic crostini, p54
Dinner	Herby artichoke casserole, p102	Sesame-crusted salmon, p88	Stir-fried tofu with prawns & rice noodles, p91
Dessert	Tropical fruit salad with green tea syrup, p121	Poached apricots with orange flower water, p125	Brazil nut & banana parfait, p110

WEEK 2

Thursday	Friday	Saturday	Sunday
Banana oat smoothie, p39	Baked eggs with spinach, p43	Potato & sweetcorn hash with frazzled eggs, p46	Butternut squash & ricotta frittata, p48
Olive & sun-dried tomato scones, p64	Sesame snaps, p55	Smoked salmon & avocado cornets, p56	Fig & apricot flapjacks, p58
Broccoli & almond soup, p70	Rare beef & baby beetroot salad, p76	Minted kale soup, p68	Turkey soup with lemon & barley, p69
½ papaya	Blueberry & mint smoothie, p60	Strawberry & banana muffins, p59	White bean hummus with pitta bites, p50
Thai turkey burgers with kale crisps, p98	Red mullet with capers & warm tomato salad, p92	Penne with tomato, artichoke & olive sauce, p104	Thai beef & mixed pepper stir-fry, p100
Watermelon, ginger & lime granita, p108	Orange, ginger & sesame rice pudding, p122	Chocolate dipped fruit, p124	Fig & grape tarts, p120

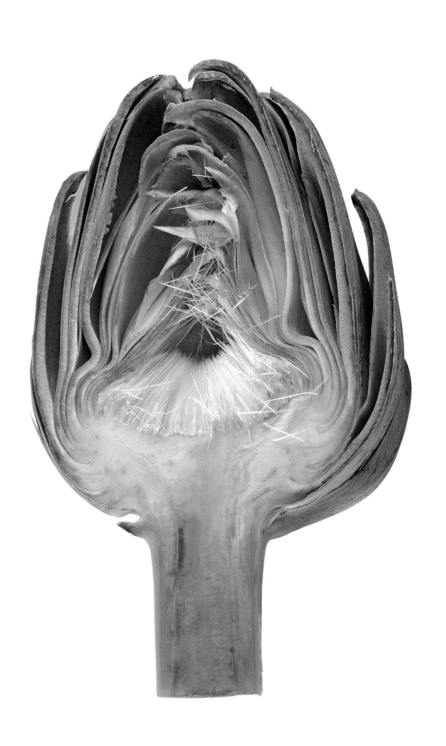

HAPPY
RECIPES

STRAWBERRY, WATERMELON & MINT SMOOTHIE

This fresh-tasting, antioxidant-rich smoothie is perfect for a quick breakfast or nourishing snack.

Preparation time: 5 minutes
Serves 4
....

16 large **strawberries**, hulled,
   plus 2 more, halved,
   to garnish
1 medium **watermelon**,
   peeled and deseeded
3 tbsps chopped **mint**
100 ml (3½ fl oz) **papaya juice**
mint sprigs, to garnish

Place all the ingredients in a blender or food processor and blend until smooth.
....

Divide the smoothie mixture between 4 glasses. Garnish with half a strawberry and a mint sprig. Serve immediately.
....

MUESLI WITH PEACHES & YOGURT

This sweet, satisfying muesli contains a host of anxiety-combatting ingredients.

Preparation time: 15 minutes, plus soaking
Cooking time: 5 minutes (optional)
Serves 4

200 g (7 oz) **porridge oats**
50 g (2 oz) **wheatgerm**
50 g (2 oz) **sunflower seeds**
25 g (1 oz) **sesame seeds** or **linseeds**
50 g (2 oz) **pumpkin seeds**
50 g (2 oz) **almonds**
50 g (2 oz) **hazelnuts**
75 g (3 oz) soft **dried apricots**, chopped
50 g (2 oz) **dried cranberries**
50 g (2 oz) **golden raisins**
350 ml (12 fl oz) **peach** or **white grape juice**
350 ml (12 fl oz) **live Greek yogurt**
2 **peaches**, peeled, stoned and sliced

Place the porridge oats in a large bowl and stir in the wheatgerm, seeds, nuts and dried fruits. Add the juice and leave to soak for at least 4 hours, or overnight.

When all of the juice has been absorbed, divide between 4 serving bowls and top with the yogurt and sliced peaches. Serve immediately.

If you prefer a warm breakfast, transfer the soaked muesli to a saucepan and cook over a low heat, stirring frequently, for about 5 minutes until heated through. Serve with the yogurt and peaches.

BANANA OAT SMOOTHIE

This smoothie is unbelievably filling, perfect for a speedy breakfast before a busy day.

Preparation time: 5 minutes
Serves 4
....

100 g (3½ oz) **coarse oatmeal**
475 ml (16 fl oz) **live natural yogurt**
4 **bananas**, roughly chopped
475 ml (16 fl oz) **skimmed milk** or **rice milk**
3 tbsps runny **honey**
1 tsp **ground cinnamon**

Place all the ingredients in a blender or food processor and blend until smooth then divide between 4 large glasses to serve.
....

To vary the flavour from time to time, add a handful of pecan nuts and substitute maple syrup for the honey.
....

NUTTY PASSION FRUIT YOGURT

This nutty, seed-rich yogurt will help to balance your moods and boost energy levels for the day ahead.

Preparation time: 10 minutes
Serves 4
....

seeds and pulp from 4 **passion fruit**
475 ml (16 fl oz) **live natural yogurt**
8 tbsps clear **wild honey**
100 g (3½ oz) **hazelnuts**,
   toasted and roughly chopped
50 g (2 oz) **brazil nuts**, roughly chopped
50 g (2 oz) **sunflower seeds**
8 **clementines**, peeled and chopped

Place the passion fruit seeds and pulp into a large bowl. Add the yogurt and mix together gently.
....

Put 1 tbsp of the honey in each of 4 narrow glasses and scatter with half the nuts and half the sunflower seeds. Spoon half the yogurt over the nuts and arrange half the clementine pieces on top.
....

Repeat the layering, reserving a few of the nuts for decoration. Scatter the nuts over the top and chill until ready to serve.
....

APPLE & CRANBERRY GRANOLA

The oats in this tasty breakfast granola will set you up for the day and help to establish a feeling of calm.

Preparation time: 15 minutes
Cooking time: 15–30 minutes
Serves 12
·················

2 large **apples**, peeled, cored and chopped
4 tbsps **maple syrup**
2 tsps **ground cinnamon**
2 tbsps **olive oil**
1 tsp grated **nutmeg**
250 g (8 oz) **porridge oats**
25 g (1 oz) **golden linseeds**
50 g (2 oz) **almonds**, crushed
50 g (2 oz) **brazil nuts**, crushed
50 g (2 oz) **pecans**, crushed
50 g (2 oz) **sunflower seeds**
150 g (5 oz) **dried cranberries**

To serve
125 ml (4 fl oz) **live natural yogurt** per serving
handful of fresh fruit (**grapes, blueberries or sliced peach**) per serving

Place the apples, maple syrup, cinnamon, olive oil and nutmeg in a blender or food processor and blend until smooth.
···

Place the oats, linseeds, almonds, brazil nuts, pecans and sunflower seeds in a large bowl, add the apple mixture and stir until well coated.
···································

Spread out on a lightly greased baking sheet and cook in a preheated oven, 160°C (325°F), Gas Mark 3, for 15–30 minutes, stirring frequently until it turns golden brown and no steam rises when you stir it. Remove from the oven, allow to cool and stir in the cranberries.
··

The granola can be stored in an airtight container for up to 3 weeks. Serve topped with yogurt and fresh fruit.
···

BAKED EGGS WITH SPINACH

This rich, delicious breakfast dish is bursting with nutrients and ideal for a lazy weekend morning.

Preparation time: 15 minutes
Cooking time: 25 minutes
Serves 4
....

1 tbsp **unsalted butter**,
    plus extra for greasing
½ **onion**, finely chopped
500 g (1 lb) **spinach**, coarsely chopped
4 tbsps **double cream** or **live Greek yogurt**
½ tsp grated **nutmeg**
4 **eggs**
sea salt and **black pepper**

To serve
wholemeal toast
unsmoked turkey bacon

Heat the butter in a large saucepan, add the onion and cook over a medium heat until just beginning to brown at the edges. Tip in the spinach and cook for 5 minutes, stirring frequently, until wilted. Remove from the heat and season to taste.

....

Divide the spinach mixture between 4 greased ramekins, about 7.5 cm (3 in) in diameter. Drizzle the cream over the spinach, sprinkle with nutmeg and top each ramekin with an egg, taking care not to break the yolks.

....

Season to taste and place in a preheated oven, 200°C (400°F), Gas Mark 6, for 12-15 minutes, or until the egg whites have just set. Serve with wholemeal toast and unsmoked turkey bacon.

....

EGGS BENEDICT WITH SMOKED SALMON

This is an excellent start to the day, stabilizing blood sugar, lifting your mood and reducing stress hormones.

Preparation time: 10 minutes
Cooking time: 20 minutes
Serves 4
....

2 tbsps **tarragon vinegar**
4 large **eggs**
4 **wholemeal English muffins**,
   split and toasted
8 small slices of **smoked salmon**
snipped **chives**, to garnish

Tarragon hollandaise
250 ml (8 fl oz) **live natural yogurt**
3 **egg yolks**
2 tsps **lemon juice**
finely grated rind of ½ **lemon**
½ tsp **sea salt**
2 tsps finely chopped **tarragon**
½ tsp **Dijon mustard**
black pepper

To make the hollandaise sauce, place the yogurt, egg yolks and lemon juice in a heatproof bowl, stir well and set over a saucepan of gently simmering water, taking care not to let the water touch the bottom of the bowl.

....

Stir vigorously for about 15 minutes as the sauce heats and thickens. Stir in the lemon rind, salt, tarragon and mustard, and season to taste with pepper. Remove from the heat and set aside.

....

Bring a saucepan of water to the boil, add the vinegar and reduce the heat to a slow simmer. One by one, crack the eggs into the water and cook for 3-4 minutes, or until the whites are firm but the yolks still runny.

....

Divide the toasted muffin halves between 4 serving plates and top with the salmon. Arrange the poached eggs on top and drizzle with the hollandaise sauce. Garnish with snipped chives and serve immediately.

....

POTATO & SWEETCORN HASH WITH FRAZZLED EGGS

This dish will satisfy the heartiest appetite, sustaining energy and encouraging relaxation even at the most stressful times.

Preparation time: 15 minutes
Cooking time: 30 minutes
Serves 4
....

750 g (1½ lb) **potatoes**, peeled and diced
2 tbsps **olive oil**
1 large **onion**, finely chopped
1 large **green pepper**, cored, deseeded and chopped
1 tsp **smoked paprika**
200 g (7 oz) can **sweetcorn**, drained
olive oil spray
4 large **eggs**
2 tbsps snipped **chives**
sea salt and **black pepper**

Cook the potatoes in a large saucepan of lightly salted boiling water for 12–15 minutes until tender, then drain in a colander.
....

Meanwhile, heat the oil in a large nonstick, ovenproof frying pan over a medium heat. Add the onion and green pepper and cook, stirring occasionally, for 7–8 minutes until softened and lightly golden.
....

Add the cooked potatoes, smoked paprika and sweetcorn, season generously and cook for 3–4 minutes, stirring frequently. Slide the pan under a preheated hot grill, keeping the handle away from the heat, and grill for 2–3 minutes until crispy.
....

Meanwhile, spray a large frying pan with olive oil spray and place over a medium heat until very hot. Crack the eggs into the pan and fry for 3 minutes until the whites are set and crispy.
....

Serve the eggs immediately with the potato and sweetcorn hash, sprinkled with the chives.
....

COURGETTE & STILTON FRITTERS

Rich in antioxidants and folic acid, these moreish fritters make a great breakfast or starter dish.

Preparation time: 10 minutes
Cooking time: 20 minutes
Serves 4

2 tbsps **olive oil**
1 large **courgette**, finely chopped
3 **eggs**
150 ml (¼ pint) **milk**
150 g (5 oz) **self-raising flour**, sifted
400 g (13 oz) can **flageolet beans**,
    drained and rinsed
handful of **parsley**, chopped
3 spring **onions**, chopped
325 g (11 oz) can **sweetcorn**, drained
100 g (3½ oz) **Stilton cheese**, crumbled
sea salt and **black pepper**
poached eggs, to serve

Heat half the oil in a nonstick frying pan, add the courgette and fry for 3–4 minutes until golden and tender.

Beat together the eggs, milk and flour in a bowl, then stir in the beans, parsley, spring onions, sweetcorn, Stilton and the cooked courgette. Season to taste.

Heat the remaining oil in the frying pan and add tbsps of the mixture to the pan, a few at a time. Gently flatten each fritter with the back of a fork and fry for 1–2 minutes on each side until golden.

Repeat with the remaining mixture, keeping the cooked fritters warm in a low oven while you finish cooking the rest. Serve with poached eggs.

BUTTERNUT SQUASH & RICOTTA FRITTATA

This filling, balancing frittata makes a nice weekend breakfast served with wholemeal toast.

Preparation time: 10 minutes
Cooking time: 30 minutes
Serves 4
....

1 tbsp **extra virgin rapeseed oil**
1 red **onion**, thinly sliced
450 g (14½ oz) **butternut squash**,
    peeled and diced
8 **eggs**
1 tbsp chopped **thyme**
2 tbsps chopped **sage**
125 g (4 oz) **ricotta cheese**
sea salt and **black pepper**
wholemeal toast, to serve (optional)

Heat the oil in a large nonstick, ovenproof frying pan over a medium-low heat, and add the onion and butternut squash. Cover loosely and cook gently, stirring frequently, for 18–20 minutes or until tender and golden.
....

Beat the eggs lightly with the thyme, sage and ricotta, then season generously and pour over the butternut squash. Cook for a further 2–3 minutes until the egg is almost set, stirring occasionally to prevent the base from burning.
....

Slide the pan under a preheated grill, keeping the handle away from the heat, and grill for 3–4 minutes, or until the egg is set and the frittata is golden. Cut into wedges and serve with wholemeal toast, if desired.
....

WHITE BEAN HUMMUS WITH PITTA BITES

This bean hummus makes a pleasant change from the traditional chickpeas and it's equally nutritious.

Preparation time: 10 minutes
Serves 12
....

400 g (13 oz) can **cannellini** or **butter beans**
125 g (4 oz) **tahini**
100 ml (3½ fl oz) **lemon juice**
finely grated rind of 1 **lemon**
1 **garlic clove**, crushed
pinch of **sea salt**
2 tbsps **olive oil**
2 tbsps chopped **parsley** (optional)
1 **wholemeal pitta bread** per serving,
    toasted and cut into fingers

Drain the beans, reserving 2 tbsps of liquid from the can, and place in a blender or food processor with the tahini, lemon juice and rind, garlic and salt. Blend until smooth then, while the motor is still running, add half the olive oil and a little of the reserved liquid if the mixture is too thick.

....

Transfer to a serving bowl and drizzle over the remaining olive oil. Sprinkle with the chopped parsley, if liked, and serve with toasted pitta fingers. The hummus can be stored in an airtight container in the refrigerator for up to 3 days.

....

MACKEREL PÂTÉ ON RYE CRISPS

Bursting with brain-nourishing omega-3 oils, this delicious pâté is an excellent way to add fish to the diet.

Preparation time: 15 minutes
Serves 4
....

4 **smoked mackerel fillets**,
   skin and bones removed
50 g (2 oz) **cream cheese**
100 g (3½ oz) **mascarpone cheese**
100 g (3½ oz) **crème fraîche**
1 tsp chopped **dill**, plus extra to garnish
4 tsps hot **horseradish sauce**
finely grated rind and juice of 1 **lemon**
black pepper

To serve
4 thin slices of **dark rye bread**, toasted
red chicory leaves

Place 3 of the mackerel fillets, the cream cheese, mascarpone, crème fraîche, dill, horseradish and lemon rind in a blender or food processor and blend until smooth.
....

Transfer the mixture to a serving bowl, flake the remaining mackerel and add to the bowl with the lemon juice. Season with pepper and stir to combine.
....

Serve with rye toast and red chicory leaves for scooping. The pâté can be stored in an airtight container in the refrigerator for up to 2 days.
....

ROASTED GARLIC CROSTINI

Eat these crunchy garlicky bites plain or top with basil leaves, tomatoes, tapenade, avocado or roasted peppers.

Preparation time: 10 minutes
Cooking time: 45 minutes
Serves 4
....

4 heads of **garlic**
4 tbsps **olive oil**
1 tsp **lemon** juice
8 thin slices of **light rye**
    or **wholemeal bread**
sea salt and **black pepper**

Place the garlic heads in a roasting pan and drizzle with half the olive oil. Place in a preheated oven, 190°C (375°F), Gas Mark 5, for 45 minutes–1 hour, or until the cloves are soft.

....

About 15 minutes before the end of cooking time, brush the bread with the remaining olive oil, arrange on a baking sheet and place in the oven with the garlic until golden and crisp.

....

Remove the garlic from the oven and cut the heads in half horizontally. Squeeze or scoop out the soft pulp into a bowl. Add any olive oil from the pan, season to taste and stir in the lemon juice. Mash to a smooth purée and spread on the crostini. Serve hot or cold.

....

SESAME SNAPS

While these little snaps are high in sugar, the sesame seeds make them highly nutritious – but stick to one or two!

Preparation time: 5 minutes, plus cooling
Cooking time: 10 minutes
Makes 24

....

200 g (7 oz) toasted **sesame seeds**
75 g (3 oz) **brown sugar**
250 ml (8 fl oz) **wild honey**

Place all the ingredients in a heavy-based saucepan over a medium heat and bring to the boil. Reduce the heat and cook gently, stirring frequently, for 8–10 minutes, or until the mixture becomes thick, syrupy and a slightly darker brown.

....

Pour the mixture on a baking sheet lined with nonstick baking paper, spread out evenly with a palette knife and smooth the surface. Allow to cool for a few minutes, then cut into pieces. Allow to cool completely before serving.

....

The sesame snaps can be stored in an airtight container for up to 2 weeks.

....

SMOKED SALMON & AVOCADO CORNETS

Salmon and avocado boost happiness, while nori promotes the health of the thyroid, which governs energy levels.

Preparation time: 25 minutes,
   plus draining, standing and cooling
Cooking time: 15 minutes
Serves 4
....

200 g (7 oz) **sushi rice**
250 ml (8 fl oz) **water**
75 ml (3 fl oz) **Japanese rice vinegar**
2 tbsps **caster sugar**
½ tsp **salt**
6 sheets of **nori seaweed**, quartered
250 g (8 oz) **smoked salmon**, cut into strips
1 **avocado**, peeled, stoned, sliced
   and drizzled with lemon juice
½ tsp **wasabi paste**
1 tbsp **Japanese pickled ginger**
handful of baby **watercress** leaves

To serve
wasabi (Japanese horseradish) paste
shoyu (Japanese soy sauce)

Place the rice in a large bowl, cover with cold water and stir it, using your fingers. Drain and repeat 2 or 3 times until the water becomes clear. Leave to drain in a fine sieve for at least 30 minutes.
....

Place the rice and measurement water in a heavy-based saucepan over a medium heat and bring to the boil. Reduce the heat, cover and cook for 12 minutes until tender. Remove the pan from the heat and stand, covered, for 15 minutes.
....

Mix the rice vinegar, sugar and salt in a bowl. Spread the rice on a flat plate, sprinkle with the vinegar mixture and stir it in. Cover with a damp cloth and leave to cool.
....

Make the cornets by spreading a little of the rice on each of the squares of nori and arranging a piece of salmon and a slice of avocado on top. Add a smear of wasabi and a little ginger and watercress, then roll into cornets, wetting the edge of the nori with a little water to make it stick. Serve with a bowl each of shoyu and wasabi paste for dipping.
....

FIG & APRICOT FLAPJACKS

These chewy flapjacks are packed with nutrients and plenty of slow-release carbohydrates to ward off hunger.

Preparation time: 10 minutes
Cooking time: 30 minutes
Makes 12
....

175 g (6 oz) **butter**
100 g (3½ oz) **golden caster sugar**
175 ml (6 fl oz) **maple syrup**
200 g (7 oz) **porridge oats**
50 g (2 oz) soft **dried apricots**, chopped
25 g (1 oz) **ground almonds**
25 g (1 oz) **almonds**, chopped
100 g (3½ oz) **sultanas** or **raisins**
2 tsps **sesame seeds**
1 tsp **ground cinnamon**
6 ripe **figs**, thinly sliced

Place 150 g (5 oz) of the butter, the sugar and the maple syrup in a large saucepan over a medium heat and cook until the butter has melted and the mixture begins to bubble.
....

Stir in the oats, apricots, almonds, sultanas, sesame seeds and cinnamon and stir to combine.
....

Transfer the mixture to a greased baking sheet and press down to make an even layer at least 1cm (½ in) thick. Scatter the figs over the top and dot with the remaining butter.
....

Place in a preheated oven, 180°C (350°F), Gas Mark 4, for 25 minutes, or until lightly golden. Allow to cool on the baking sheet, then cut into 12 squares. Store in an airtight container for up to a week.
....

STRAWBERRY & BANANA MUFFINS

These moist muffins contain wholemeal flour to stabilize blood sugar and are perfect for a snack or for breakfast.

Preparation time: 10 minutes
Cooking time: 20 minutes
Makes 12
....

2 **eggs**, lightly beaten
100 g (3½ oz) **apple purée**
4 tbsps **canola oil**
175 g (6 oz) dark soft **brown sugar**
2 tsps **vanilla extract**
2 tsps **ground cinnamon**,
    plus extra for dusting
¼ tsp **sea salt**
3 very ripe **bananas**, mashed
250 g (8 oz) **wholemeal flour**
1 tsp **bicarbonate of soda**
½ tsp **baking powder**
250 g (8 oz) fresh or frozen
    strawberries, sliced

Place the eggs in a large bowl with the apple purée, canola oil, sugar, vanilla, cinnamon, salt and bananas and stir until well combined.

Mix the flour with the bicarbonate of soda and baking powder in a separate bowl, then add to the banana mixture and stir to just combine, taking care not to overmix or the muffins will be tough. Lightly fold in the strawberries.

Spoon the mixture into a 12-hole muffin tin lined with paper cases and sprinkle each muffin with a little cinnamon.

Place in a preheated oven, 190°C (375°F), Gas Mark 5, for 20 minutes, or until the muffins are golden and risen. Remove from the tin and cool on a wire rack. The muffins can be stored in an airtight container for up to 4 days.

BLUEBERRY & MINT SMOOTHIE

Smoothies are quick and easy snacks and also make a nourishing breakfast when you are in a rush.

Preparation time: 10 minutes
Serves 4

....

large bunch of **mint**
400 g (13 oz) frozen **blueberries**
600 ml (1 pint) **soya milk**

Remove the leaves from the bunch of mint and reserve a few for decoration. Place the remaining leaves with the blueberries and soya milk in a blender or food processor and blend until smooth.

....

Pour the mixture into 4 tall glasses, decorate with the reserved mint leaves and serve immediately.

....

BANANA SUNFLOWER SEED COOKIES

You could exchange half the sunflower seeds in these mood-lifting cookies for the same weight of dark chocolate.

Preparation time: 10 minutes, plus chilling
Cooking time: 15 minutes
Makes 36

....

200 g (7 oz) **plain flour**
1 tsp **bicarbonate of soda**
2 very ripe **bananas**, mashed
125 g (4 oz) **butter**, softened
100 g (3½ oz) **light soft brown sugar**
1 tsp **vanilla extract**
125 g (4 oz) **sunflower seeds**

Place the flour and bicarbonate of soda in a bowl, mix to combine, then set aside. Place the bananas, butter, sugar and vanilla in a large bowl and beat until fluffy and combined.

....

Fold in the flour mixture, a little at a time, until well mixed, then stir in the sunflower seeds. Cover the bowl with clingfilm and chill in the refrigerator for 1 hour.

....

Place tbsps of the cookie dough, well spaced, on 2 baking sheets lined with nonstick baking paper. Place in a preheated oven, 180°C (350°F), Gas Mark 4, for about 12 minutes, or until lightly golden. Allow to cool a little on the baking sheets, then transfer to a wire rack to cool completely. The cookies can be stored in an airtight container for up to a week.

....

OLIVE & SUN-DRIED TOMATO SCONES

Because these scones are made with wholemeal flour, you won't experience an energy dip after eating them.

Preparation time: 15 minutes, plus cooling
Cooking time: 12 minutes
Makes 8
....

250 g (8 oz) **wholemeal flour**, plus extra for dusting
1 tsp **baking powder**
1 tsp **bicarbonate of soda**
75 g (3 oz) **butter**, cubed
25 g (1 oz) pitted **olives**, chopped
8 **sun-dried tomatoes**, chopped
1 tbsp chopped **parsley**
1 large **egg**, beaten
4 tbsps **buttermilk**, plus extra for brushing

Place the flour, baking powder, bicarbonate of soda and butter in a blender or food processor and pulse until the mixture resembles fine breadcrumbs. Alternatively, rub the butter into the flour with your fingertips.
....

Stir in the olives, tomatoes and parsley, then add the egg and buttermilk and stir with a round-bladed knife until the mixture comes together.
....

Tip the dough out on to a lightly floured surface and gently press it down to a thickness of 2.5 cm (1 inch). Use a 5 cm (2 inch) biscuit cutter to cut out the scones, rerolling the trimmings as necessary.
....

Arrange on a lightly floured baking sheet, brush with a little buttermilk and place in a preheated oven, 220°C (425°F), Gas Mark 7, for about 12 minutes until golden and risen. Transfer to a wire rack to cool.
....

LENTIL & PEA SOUP

Lentils are versatile wholegrains with a host of health benefits. Here they are combined with peas and fragrant herbs.

Preparation time: 15 minutes
Cooking time: 25 minutes
Serves 4

1 tsp **olive oil**
1 **leek**, finely sliced
1 **garlic clove**, crushed
400 g (13 oz) can **Puy lentils**,
 rinsed and drained
900 ml (1½ pints) **vegetable stock**
2 tbsps chopped **mixed herbs**,
 such as thyme, oregano,
 tarragon, mint and parsley
200 g (7 oz) **frozen peas**
2 tbsps **crème fraîche**
2 tbsps chopped **mint**
sea salt and **black pepper**

Heat the oil in a large saucepan over a medium heat, add the leek and garlic and cook for 5–6 minutes until softened.

Add the lentils, stock and herbs, bring to the boil, reduce the heat and simmer, covered, for 10 minutes. Add the peas and continue to cook for 5 minutes.

Remove from the heat, allow to cool a little, then transfer half the soup to a blender or food processor and blend until smooth. Return to the pan, stir to combine with the unblended soup, then heat through and season to taste.

Stir together the crème fraîche and mint. Ladle the soup into warmed bowls and serve immediately with the crème fraîche on the side.

MINTED KALE SOUP

This warm, buttery soup is filling and positively bursting with nutrients to nourish, soothe and heal.

Preparation time: 15 minutes
Cooking time: 30 minutes
Serves 4
....

2 tbsps **butter**
2 tbsps **olive oil**
1 large **onion**, chopped
2 **garlic cloves**, chopped
3 **potatoes**, peeled and chopped
400 g (13 oz) can **butter beans**,
    rinsed and drained
1.2 litres (2 pints) **chicken**
    or **vegetable stock**
300 g (10 oz) **kale**, shredded
    and thick stems removed
4 tbsps chopped **mint**, plus
    a few whole leaves to garnish
sea salt and **black pepper**

To serve
rye toast or **spelt bread**, to serve
6 tbsps **live natural yogurt**
    or **crème fraîche** (optional)

Heat the butter and oil in a large saucepan over a medium heat and add the onion. Cook for about 5 minutes until starting to soften, then add the garlic and potatoes.
....

Stir in the beans and stock, bring to the boil, reduce the heat and simmer for about 15 minutes, stirring and skimming frequently. Add the kale and mint and continue cooking for a further 5 minutes until the vegetables are tender.
....

Remove from the heat, cool slightly, then transfer to a blender or food processor and blend until smooth. Season to taste and ladle the soup into warmed bowls. Garnish with mint leaves and serve with rye toast or spelt bread, and a swirl of yogurt or crème fraîche, if liked.
....

TURKEY SOUP WITH LEMON & BARLEY

This warming soup is surprisingly light and full of nutrient-rich, energy-boosting barley and calming turkey.

Preparation time: 15 minutes
Cooking time: 40 minutes
Serves 4
....

2 tbsps **olive oil**
1 large **onion**, finely chopped
3 **garlic cloves**, finely chopped
1 tsp **ground turmeric**
½ tsp **ground cinnamon**
½ tsp **ground cumin**
½ tsp **ground cardamom**
1 cm (½ in) piece of fresh **root ginger**, peeled and finely chopped
finely grated rind and juice of 2 **lemons**
1.2 litres (2 pints) **chicken** or **vegetable stock**
150 g (5 oz) **pearl barley**
300 g (10 oz) **cooked turkey**, shredded
75 g (3 oz) fresh **coriander**, chopped, plus extra to garnish
sea salt and **black pepper**

Heat the oil in a large saucepan over a medium-low heat, add the onion and cook gently until softened and just beginning to brown. Stir in the garlic and cook for another minute, and then add the turmeric, cinnamon, cumin, cardamom and ginger.
....

Add the lemon rind and juice, and the stock and bring to the boil. Reduce the heat to a slow simmer and add the barley. Cover and cook for about 25 minutes, stirring occasionally, until the barley is tender but still has a little bite.
....

Add the turkey and coriander and season to taste. Cook, uncovered, for a further 5 minutes, then ladle the soup into warmed bowls and garnish with chopped coriander.
....

BROCCOLI & ALMOND SOUP

This light soup provides brain-supporting omega oils as well as protection from the harmful side-effects of stress.

Preparation time: 15 minutes
Cooking time: 20 minutes
Serves 4
....

25 g (1 oz) **butter**
1 **onion**, roughly chopped
500 g (1 lb) **broccoli**, roughly chopped
40 g (1½ oz) **ground almonds**
900 ml (1½ pints) **vegetable** or
    chicken stock
2 tsps **dried thyme**
300 ml (½ pint) **milk**
sea salt and **black pepper**

To serve
15 g (½ oz) **butter**
25 g (1 oz) **almonds**, crushed
6 tbsps **live natural yogurt**

Heat the butter in a large saucepan over a medium heat, add the onion and cook gently for 5 minutes until just beginning to soften. Stir in the broccoli until coated in the butter then add the ground almonds, stock and thyme and season to taste.

....

Bring to the boil, reduce the heat and simmer, covered, for 10 minutes until the broccoli is just tender and still bright green.

....

Meanwhile, for the garnish, heat the butter in a frying pan, add the almonds and fry for a few minutes, stirring constantly, until golden.

....

Remove the soup from the heat, allow to cool a little, then transfer in batches to a blender or food processor and blend until finely speckled with green. Pour the soup back into the saucepan and stir in the milk. Reheat and season to taste.

....

Ladle the soup into warmed bowls, drizzle with the yogurt and sprinkle with the almonds. Serve immediately.

....

MISO BROTH WITH PRAWNS

With prawns to boost immunity, libido and virility, this easy recipe will become a lunchtime standby on busy days.

Preparation time: 10 minutes
Cooking time: 10 minutes
Serves 6
....

4 spring **onions** or **baby leeks**, thinly sliced
1.5 cm (¾ inch) piece of fresh **root ginger**,
    finely chopped
½–1 large **red chilli**, deseeded
    and thinly sliced
1.5 litres (2½ pints) **fish** or **vegetable stock**
3 tbsps **miso paste**
2 tbsps **mirin** (Japanese cooking wine)
1 tbsp **dark soy sauce**
100 g (3½ oz) **pak choi**, thinly sliced
2 tbsps chopped fresh **coriander**
150 g (5 oz) cooked peeled **prawns**
1 small **avocado**, peeled, stoned
    and chopped

Place the white parts of the spring onions or leeks into a saucepan with the ginger, chilli, stock, miso, mirin and soy sauce. Bring to the boil, reduce the heat and simmer for 5 minutes.

....

Stir in the green parts of the spring onions or leeks, the pak choi, coriander and prawns and cook for 2–3 minutes or until the pak choi has just wilted. Ladle the soup into warmed bowls and sprinkle with the chopped avocado. Serve immediately.

....

GOATS' CHEESE, APPLE & BROCCOLI SALAD

With a host of mood-lifting nutrients, this salad is ideal as a warming lunch or a starter for a special dinner.

Preparation time: 20 minutes
Cooking time: 5 minutes
Serves 4
....

1 tbsp **olive oil**, plus extra for brushing
1 tbsp **lemon juice**
1 tsp **dried thyme**
100 g (3½ oz) **mixed salad leaves**
1 head of **broccoli**, cut into small florets
2 **Granny Smith apples**, peeled, cored and thinly sliced
2 **goats' cheese** logs, cut into 1 cm (½ inch) slices
4 tbsps **Manuka honey**
sea salt and **black pepper**

Mix the olive oil, lemon juice and thyme in a small bowl and season to taste. Arrange the salad leaves, broccoli and half the apple slices on a large platter, drizzle with the dressing and toss until coated.

....

Place the goats' cheese on a lightly greased baking sheet and brush with a little olive oil. Place in a preheated oven, 200°C (400°F), Gas Mark 6, for about 5 minutes or until just starting to brown.

....

Meanwhile, place the honey and remaining apple in a food processor or blender and blend until smooth. Transfer to a small saucepan and heat for 2–3 minutes, until just warm.

....

Arrange the warm cheese on the salad and drizzle with the honey mixture. Sprinkle with black pepper and serve immediately.

....

FIG, RASPBERRY & PROSCIUTTO SALAD

Sweet and salty, this fresh salad is quick to make, and provides a boost of fibre, antioxidants and protein.

Preparation time: 5 minutes
Serves 4
....

150 g (5 oz) **rocket and leaf beet salad**
6 ripe **figs**, halved
150 g (5 oz) **raspberries**
8 slices of **prosciutto**
2 tbsps aged **balsamic vinegar**
2 tbsps **olive oil**
300 g (10 oz) **buffalo mozzarella**

Arrange the salad leaves on a large serving plate with the figs, raspberries and prosciutto. Whisk the vinegar and oil together to make a dressing.
....

Tear the mozzarella into large pieces and arrange on top of the salad. Drizzle the dressing on top and serve immediately.
....

RARE BEEF & BABY BEETROOT SALAD

Combined with iron-rich beef, horseradish is a natural digestive and adds piquancy to this mood-enhancing salad.

Preparation time: 20 minutes
Cooking time: 25 minutes
Serves 4

250 g (8 oz) unpeeled **baby beetroot**, stalks removed
400 g (13 oz) **lean rump** or **sirloin steak**, trimmed
2 tsps **olive oil**
finely grated rind of 1 **lemon**
1 **garlic clove**, finely chopped
2 tbsps finely snipped **chives**
175 g (6 oz) **runner beans**, sliced
10 **radishes**, thinly sliced
50 g (2 oz) **walnut** pieces
125 g (4 oz) **mixed salad leaves**
1½ tbsps **lemon juice**
1 tsp **horseradish sauce**
1 tsp clear **honey**
3 tbsps **reduced-fat soured cream**
sea salt and **black pepper**

Cook the beetroot in a saucepan of lightly salted boiling water for 15–25 minutes, depending on their size, until tender.

Meanwhile, place the steak in a shallow dish with the olive oil, lemon rind, garlic, half the chives and plenty of black pepper. Toss until the meat is well coated in the marinade.

Cook the runner beans in another saucepan of lightly salted boiling water for 1–2 minutes until almost tender. Drain and refresh in cold water.

Heat a ridged griddle pan over a medium-high heat and cook the steak for 1 minute on each side until charred but still pink inside. Set aside in a warm place to rest.

Drain the beetroot, cut into wedges and toss with the beans, radishes, walnuts and salad leaves, then heap on to serving plates.

Mix the lemon juice, horseradish, honey, soured cream and remaining chives in a bowl and season to taste. Slice the beef thinly and arrange on top of the salads, drizzle with the horseradish dressing and serve immediately.

TURKEY & PEANUT NOODLE SALAD

Both peanuts and poultry contain high-quality protein and help to boost levels of feel-good serotonin.

Preparation time: 15 minutes
Cooking time: 15 minutes
Serves 4
....

350 g (11½ oz) **brown rice noodles**
100 g (3½ oz) **sugarsnap peas**
100 g (3½ oz) **baby sweetcorn**
1 tbsp **sesame oil**
1 tsp **olive oil**
625 g (1¼ lb) boneless, skinless **turkey**, cubed
3 tbsps **sweet chilli sauce**
1 tbsp **dark soy sauce**

4 **spring onions**, finely sliced
100 g (3½ oz) **peanuts**, lightly toasted
75 g (3 oz) fresh **coriander**, roughly chopped

Dressing
1 tbsp **olive oil**
1 tbsp **Thai fish sauce**
1 tsp **hot chilli sauce**
1 tbsp **dark soy sauce**
1 **garlic clove**, finely chopped
finely grated rind and juice of 2 limes

Soak the noodles in boiling water until tender, according to packet instructions, and drain thoroughly. Meanwhile, cook the sugarsnap peas and baby sweetcorn in a saucepan of lightly salted boiling water for 2–3 minutes, then drain and refresh in cold water.

....

Heat a large frying pan or wok over a medium heat and add the oils, followed by the turkey. Cook, stirring often, until golden. Add the sweet chilli sauce and soy sauce and continue cooking for 4–5 minutes, or until the turkey is cooked through.

....

Place all the dressing ingredients in a screw-top jar and shake vigorously until well combined. Arrange the noodles, sugarsnap peas and sweetcorn in a large bowl, drizzle with the dressing and toss to coat.

....

Place the spring onions, peanuts, coriander and turkey on top and toss lightly again. Serve warm or at room temperature.

....

BEETROOT, GRAPE & FETA SALAD

With tangy grapes, salty feta and sweet beetroot, this is antioxidant heaven, designed to promote overall wellbeing.

Preparation time: 20 minutes
Cooking time: 25 minutes
Serves 4

8 large **beetroot**, peeled
and cut into chunks
2 tbsps **olive oil**
150 g (5 oz) **grapes**, halved
100 g (3½ oz) **mixed salad leaves**
4 **spring onions**, finely sliced
2 tbsps **walnut oil**
2 tbsps **balsamic vinegar**
1 tsp **dried thyme**
150 g (5 oz) **feta cheese**, crumbled
50 g (2 oz) **pine nuts**, lightly toasted
sea salt and **black pepper**

Place the beetroot chunks on a nonstick baking sheet, drizzle with the olive oil and season to taste. Use your hands to toss the beetroot in the oil until evenly coated.

Place in a preheated oven, 200°C (400°F), Gas Mark 6, for about 25 minutes, turning once or twice. About 10 minutes before the end of cooking, add half the grapes and cook until just starting to brown.

Arrange the salad leaves on 4 serving plates and sprinkle with the spring onions. Mix the walnut oil, balsamic vinegar and thyme in a small bowl and season to taste.

Remove the beetroot and grapes from the oven and allow to cool slightly. Arrange on the salad leaves, sprinkle with the remaining grapes, the feta and pine nuts and lightly toss. Drizzle with the balsamic dressing and serve immediately.

SALAD NIÇOISE WITH ARTICHOKES & ASPARAGUS

This satisfying salad contains enough protein to keep blood sugar levels stable and appetites fully sated.

Preparation time: 15 minutes
Cooking time: 2 minutes
Serves 4
....

12–16 **asparagus** spears, trimmed
1 large **romaine lettuce**, coarsely shredded
4 hard-boiled **eggs**, shelled and quartered
12 **artichoke hearts** from a jar, halved
200 g (7 oz) can **tuna** in water,
    drained and flaked
16 **black olives**, pitted
16 **cherry tomatoes**, halved
1 large **avocado**, peeled,
    stoned and chopped
wholemeal bread, to serve (optional)

Dressing
4 tbsps **red wine vinegar**
1 tsp **Dijon mustard**
125 ml (4 fl oz) **olive oil**
2 **garlic cloves**, crushed
1 tsp **dried thyme**
1 tsp **wild honey**
sea salt and **black pepper**

Cook the asparagus in a steamer over a saucepan of gently simmering water for 2 minutes, then refresh in cold water. Place all the dressing ingredients in a screw-top jar and shake vigorously until well combined.

Arrange the lettuce in a large bowl or serving platter and place the eggs, artichokes, tuna, olives, tomatoes, avocado, parsley and asparagus on top.

Drizzle with the dressing and toss lightly until well coated. Serve with warm, crusty wholemeal bread, if liked.

TOMATO, TOFU & HOT PEPPER SALAD

Soya is an excellent hormone balancer, while hot peppers are both warming and good for the digestion.

Preparation time: 10 minutes
Serves 4
....

4 **beefsteak tomatoes**, thinly sliced
250 g (8 oz) **tofu**, crumbled
100 g (3½ oz) **hot piquanté peppers**
  from a jar, drained and thinly sliced
6 tbsps snipped **chives**
4 tbsps chopped **flat leaf parsley**
50 g (2 oz) **pine nuts**, toasted
75 g (3 oz) **sultanas**
8 tbsps **olive oil**
4 tbsps **lemon juice**
4 tsps **caster sugar**
sea salt and **black pepper**
wholegrain bread, to serve (optional)

Arrange the tomato slices on 4 serving plates, lightly seasoning to taste. Place the tofu in a mixing bowl with the peppers, chives, parsley, pine nuts and sultanas and toss together.
....

Whisk the olive oil with the lemon juice and sugar in a small bowl, season lightly and stir into the tofu mixture. Spoon the tofu mixture over the tomatoes and serve with wholegrain bread, if liked.
....

WARM RAINBOW SALAD

Delicious, fragrant and teeming with nutrients, this lovely warm salad is packed with lots of different vegetables.

Preparation time: 20 minutes
Cooking time: 20–25 minutes
Serves 4
....

300 g (10 oz) **baby new potatoes**
1 **red pepper**, cored, deseeded and sliced
1 **yellow pepper**, cored, deseeded
 and sliced
1 tbsp **olive oil**
1 tbsp chopped **thyme**
1 large **beetroot**, peeled and coarsely grated
1 large **carrot**, coarsely grated
1 large **avocado**, peeled, stoned
 and chopped
150 g (5 oz) colourful **mixed salad leaves**
4 tbsps crushed **walnuts**
sea salt and **black pepper**

Dressing
2 tbsps **walnut oil**
1 tbsp **shallot vinegar**
1 tbsp **Dijon mustard**
pinch of **sugar**

Place the potatoes and peppers in a large roasting tin, drizzle with the olive oil and thyme and season to taste. Toss to coat the vegetables in the oil, then place in a preheated oven, 190°C (375°F), Gas Mark 5, for 20–25 minutes until tender.
....

Meanwhile, toss the beetroot, carrot and avocado with the salad leaves and divide among 4 serving plates. Place all the dressing ingredients in a screw-top jar, season to taste and shake vigorously to combine.
....

Arrange the warm vegetables on the plates on top of the salads and drizzle with the dressing. Scatter over the walnuts and serve immediately.
....

GINGER SCALLOPS WITH ASPARAGUS

Scallops not only boost virility, libido and immunity, but provide energy and balance blood sugar levels.

Preparation time: 10 minutes, plus marinating
Cooking time: 10 minutes
Serves 4
....

12 large **scallops**
2 **spring onions**, thinly sliced
finely grated rind of 1 **lime**
1 tbsp **ginger cordial**
2 tbsps **olive oil**, plus
  extra for drizzling
250 g (8 oz) fine **asparagus** spears
100 g (3½ oz) **samphire**
2 tbsps **lime juice**
2 large handfuls of **mixed salad leaves**
handful of **chervil**
sea salt and **black pepper**

Rinse the scallops and pat dry. Cut in half horizontally and place in a bowl with the spring onions, lime rind, ginger cordial and half the oil. Season to taste, toss well and set aside to marinate for 15 minutes.
....

Meanwhile, cook the asparagus in a steamer over a saucepan of gently simmering water for 5–8 minutes, adding the samphire for the last 2–3 minutes. Toss with the remaining oil and the lime juice, season to taste and keep warm.
....

Heat a large, nonstick frying pan until hot, add the scallops and cook for 1 minute on each side until golden and just cooked through. Add the marinade juices to the pan and remove from the heat.
....

Arrange the asparagus, samphire, salad leaves and chervil on 4 serving plates, top with the scallops and pan juices and serve immediately.
....

MACKEREL & ASPARAGUS TART

Mackerel and asparagus are nutrient-rich functional foods that lift mood and encourage healthy brain function.

Preparation time: 20 minutes, plus chilling
Cooking time: 30–40 minutes
Serves 4

8 **asparagus** spears, trimmed
250 g (8 oz) **smoked mackerel**,
  skin and bones removed
2 **eggs**
100 ml (3½ fl oz) **milk**
2 tbsps finely chopped **dill**
100 ml (3½ fl oz) **double cream**
sea salt and **black pepper**

Pastry
200 g (7 oz) **plain flour**,
  plus extra for dusting
75 g (3 oz) **butter**, chilled and diced
1 **egg**, plus 1 **egg yolk**

Knead the dough lightly for 1 minute until smooth, wrap in clingfilm and chill in the refrigerator for at least 30 minutes.

Roll out the pastry on a well-floured surface until it is about 2.5 mm (⅛ inch) thick and use to line a 25 cm (10 inch) round flan tin. Chill the pastry case for 1 hour.

Line the pastry case with nonstick baking paper, fill with baking beans or rice, then place in a preheated oven, 180°C (350°F), Gas Mark 4, for 10–12 minutes until lightly golden. Remove the baking paper and beans and cook for a further 2 minutes.

Meanwhile, steam the asparagus for 3–4 minutes, then refresh in cold water. Cut each spear into 3 pieces.

Flake the fish into the pastry case. Beat together the eggs, milk, dill and cream and season to taste. Add the asparagus and carefully pour the mixture into the pastry case. Return to the oven for 20–25 minutes until just set. Serve on warmed plates.

SESAME-CRUSTED SALMON

Sesame seeds have a powerful antidepressant effect and provide the basis for this healthy, restorative dinner.

Preparation time: 10 minutes
Cooking time: 12–15 minutes
Serves 4
....

4 tbsps **sesame seeds**
1 tsp dried **chilli flakes**
4 **salmon fillets**, about 100 g (3½ oz) each
2 tsps **olive oil**
2 **carrots**, cut into matchsticks
2 **red peppers**, cored, deseeded
    and thinly sliced
200 g (7 oz) **shiitake mushrooms**, halved
2 **pak choi**, quartered lengthways
4 **spring onions**, shredded
1 tbsp **dark soy sauce**
basmati rice, to serve

Mix the sesame seeds and chilli flakes on a plate, then press the salmon fillets into the mixture to coat.
....

Heat half the oil in a nonstick frying pan over a medium heat, add the salmon and cook for 3–4 minutes on each side until cooked through. Remove from the pan and keep warm.
....

Heat the remaining oil in the pan over a high heat, add the vegetables and stir-fry for 3–4 minutes until just cooked. Drizzle the soy sauce over the vegetables and serve with the salmon and basmati rice.
....

MACKEREL FILLETS WITH OAT TOPPING

Rich in healthy omega-3 oils, fresh mackerel fillets with a crunchy oat crust make a quick and delicious meal.

Preparation time: 15 minutes
Cooking time: 5 minutes
Serves 4
················

4 large **mackerel fillets**, boned
2 tsps **Dijon mustard**
2 tsps **horseradish sauce**
finely grated rind of ½ **lemon**
½ tsp **sea salt**
½ tsp **black pepper**
5 tbsps **porridge oats**
2 tbsps **butter**

To serve
watercress
steamed **broccoli**
lemon wedges

Place the mackerel fillets on a board, skin side down, and pat dry with kitchen paper. Mix the mustard, horseradish, lemon rind, salt and pepper in a small bowl and spread evenly over the tops of the fillets. Press the oats firmly on to the mustard mixture.
················

Heat the butter in a large frying pan over a medium heat. When it begins to foam, place the mackerel fillets in the pan, oat side down, and cook for 2–3 minutes.
················

Carefully turn the mackerel over and cook for another 1–2 minutes until cooked through. Serve the fish fillets on a bed of watercress, with broccoli and lemon wedges on the side.
················

STIR-FRIED TOFU
WITH PRAWNS & RICE NOODLES

With zinc-rich prawns, brown rice noodles and mood-lifting soya, this dish has everything you need to get happy.

Preparation time: 10 minutes, plus standing
Cooking time: 10 minutes
Serves 4
....

500 g (1 lb) **tofu**
6 tbsps **dark soy sauce**
2 tbsps clear **honey**
2 tbsps **groundnut oil**
300 g (10 oz) **spring greens**, shredded
625 g (1¼ lb) cooked **brown rice noodles**
400 g (13 oz) cooked peeled **prawns**
8 tbsps **hoisin sauce**
75 g (3 oz) fresh **coriander**, chopped

Pat the tofu dry with kitchen paper and cut into 2 cm (¾ inch) dice. Mix the soy sauce and honey together in a bowl, add the tofu and mix gently. Leave to stand for 5 minutes.

....

Drain the tofu, reserving the marinade, and pat the cubes dry with kitchen paper. Heat the oil in a large frying pan over a high heat and cook the tofu for 5 minutes, stirring frequently, until it is crisp and golden. Remove from the pan and keep warm.

....

Add the greens to the pan and cook quickly, stirring, until wilted. Return the tofu to the pan with the noodles and prawns and toss the ingredients together for 2 minutes until heated through.

....

Mix the hoisin sauce with the reserved marinade. Drizzle the liquid over the stir-fry, mix well, scatter with the coriander and serve immediately.

....

RED MULLET WITH CAPERS & WARM TOMATO SALAD

Red mullet is a light fish, rich in nutrients, which complements this stress-busting tomato salad.

Preparation time: 20 minutes
Cooking time: 10 minutes
Serves 4
....

8 small **red mullet fillets**
finely grated rind of 1 **lemon**
2 tsps baby **capers**, rinsed and drained
2 **spring onions**, finely sliced
375 g (12 oz) mixed **red** and **yellow cherry tomatoes**
150 g (5 oz) fine **green beans**, trimmed
2 **garlic cloves**, finely chopped
50 g (2 oz) can **anchovy fillets**, drained and chopped
1 tbsp **olive oil**
2 tbsps **lemon juice**
2 tbsps chopped **parsley**
sea salt and **black pepper**
caperberries, to garnish

Tear off 4 large sheets of foil and line with nonstick baking paper. Place 2 red mullet fillets on each piece of baking paper, then scatter with the lemon rind, capers and spring onions and season to taste. Fold over the paper-lined foil and scrunch the edges together to seal. Place the parcels on a large baking sheet.

....

Put the cherry tomatoes in an ovenproof dish with the green beans, garlic, anchovies, oil and lemon juice. Season to taste and mix well. Place in a preheated oven, 200°C (400°F), Gas Mark 6, for about 10 minutes until tender. Place the fish in the oven at the same time, for 8–10 minutes until the flesh flakes easily when pressed with a knife.

....

Spoon the vegetables and fish on to warmed serving plates. Sprinkle with the chopped parsley, garnish with caperberries and serve immediately.

....

CHICKEN & PEANUT STEW WITH BROWN RICE

This is a traditional Ghanaian dish with a few alterations. It's easy to make and children love it too.

Preparation time: 10 minutes
Cooking time: 30–35 minutes
Serves 4
....

1 **onion**, roughly chopped
3 **garlic cloves**, unpeeled, roughly chopped
5 cm (2 in) piece of fresh **root ginger**,
    peeled and roughly chopped
1 **red chilli**, deseeded and roughly chopped
2 tbsps **olive oil**
8 boneless, skinless **chicken thighs**,
    cut into bite-size pieces
400 g (13 oz) can **chopped tomatoes**
600 ml (1 pint) **chicken** or **vegetable stock**
4 tbsps **peanut butter**
sea salt and **black pepper**
25 g (1 oz) roasted **peanuts**, to garnish
brown rice, to serve

Place the onion, garlic, ginger and chilli in a blender or food processor and blend until smooth. Heat the oil in a large saucepan over a medium heat, add the onion mixture and cook for 2–3 minutes until fragrant.
....

Add the chicken and cook for 2–3 minutes, turning frequently, until browned all over. Stir in the tomatoes and stock and simmer, uncovered, for 15–20 minutes until the chicken is cooked through.
....

Stir in the peanut butter and cook for a further 5 minutes. Season to taste and ladle over brown rice. Serve immediately, garnished with a sprinkling of roasted peanuts.
....

CAULIFLOWER & TURKEY BIRYANI

This one-pot dish combines relaxation-inducing turkey with vitamin C-rich cauliflower.

Preparation time: 20 minutes
Cooking time: 35 minutes
Serves 4
....

300 g (10 oz) boneless, skinless **turkey** breast, cubed
1 small **cauliflower**, cut into small florets
1 **onion**, thinly sliced
4 tbsps **groundnut oil**
2 **bay leaves**
3 **cardamom pods**, crushed
300 g (10 oz) **basmati rice**
750 ml (1¼ pints) **chicken stock**
1 tbsp **nigella seeds**
sea salt and **black pepper**

Marinade
1 **onion**, roughly chopped
2 **garlic cloves**, chopped
25 g (1 oz) fresh **root ginger**, peeled and roughly chopped
2 tsps **ground turmeric**
¼ tsp **ground cloves**
½ tsp **dried chilli flakes**
¼ tsp **ground cinnamon**
2 tsps **medium curry paste**
1 tbsp **lemon juice**
2 tsps **sugar**

To garnish
1 **onion**, thinly sliced
2 tbsps **flaked almonds**, toasted

Place all the marinade ingredients in a blender or food processor and blend until smooth. Transfer to a large bowl, add the turkey, season to taste, mix well and set aside.
....

For the garnish, heat 1 tbsp of the oil in a large frying pan over a medium heat and cook the onion until golden and crisp. Remove with a slotted spoon, drain on kitchen paper and set aside.
....

Add the cauliflower to the frying pan and fry gently for 5 minutes. Add the remaining onion and cook, stirring, for about 5 minutes until the cauliflower is softened and golden. Drain on kitchen paper and set aside.
....

Heat the remaining oil in the pan. Add the turkey and marinade and cook gently for 5 minutes, stirring frequently. Add the bay leaves, cardamom, rice and stock and bring to the boil. Reduce the heat and simmer very gently, stirring occasionally, for 10–12 minutes until the rice is tender and the stock has been absorbed, adding a little water if the mixture becomes too dry.
....

Stir in the nigella seeds and cauliflower and heat through. Serve immediately, garnished with the crispy onion and almonds.
....

TURKEY, LENTIL & APRICOT STEW

This aromatic stew is easy to make and freezes well, so double the quantities for a healthy ready meal another time.

Preparation time: 15 minutes
Cooking time: 30 minutes
Serves 4
....

2 tbsps **olive oil**
1 large **onion**, finely chopped
2.5 cm (1 in) piece of fresh **root ginger**, peeled and grated
2 **garlic cloves**, finely chopped
1 tsp **black pepper**
1 tsp **ground coriander**
1 tsp **ground cinnamon**
1 tsp **ground cloves**
1 tsp **ground cumin**
½ tsp **ground cardamom**
2 tsps **paprika**
1 tsp grated **nutmeg**
500 g (1 lb) boneless, skinless **turkey**, cut into chunks
150 g (5 oz) **red lentils**
600 ml (1 pint) **vegetable** or **chicken stock**
finely grated rind and juice of 1 **lemon**
50 g (2 oz) soft **dried apricots**, diced
75 g (3 oz) fresh **coriander**, chopped

Heat the oil in a large saucepan over a medium heat, add the onion, ginger and garlic and cook for about 5 minutes, until the onion is beginning to soften.
....

Place the spices in a bowl and stir to mix. Add the turkey chunks and stir well to coat evenly. Add to the pan and cook for 5 minutes, stirring frequently, until browned all over.
....

Add the lentils and mix gently, then add the stock, lemon rind, lemon juice, apricots and half the coriander. Bring to the boil, reduce the heat and simmer for about 15 minutes, or until the turkey is cooked through and the lentils are tender. Add the remaining coriander and ladle into big bowls to serve.
....

THAI TURKEY BURGERS WITH KALE CRISPS

These flavoursome burgers are ideal for relaxed family meals and offer a good hit of mood-lifting tryptophan.

Preparation time: 20 minutes
Cooking time: 20 minutes
Serves 4

400 g (13 oz) **minced turkey thigh** meat
4 **spring onions**, finely chopped
1 cm (½ in) piece of fresh **root ginger**, peeled and grated
1 **garlic clove**, crushed
1 **lemon grass stalk**, outer leaves removed and core finely chopped
½ **red chilli**, deseeded and finely chopped
2 tbsps finely chopped fresh **coriander**
1 **egg**, lightly beaten
4 **wholemeal buns**
sea salt and **black pepper**

Kale crisps
300 g (10 oz) **kale**, washed and cut into bite-size pieces
finely grated rind of 1 **lemon**
1 tbsp **olive oil**
sesame seeds, for sprinkling (optional)

To make the kale crisps, place the kale in a large bowl and toss with the lemon rind, olive oil and a little sea salt. Arrange in a single layer on 1 or 2 baking sheets.

Place in a preheated oven, 200°C (400°F), Gas Mark 6, for 15–20 minutes, turning halfway through cooking time, until crunchy and crisp. Sprinkle with a little more salt or some sesame seeds, if liked.

Meanwhile, place the turkey in a large bowl with the onions, ginger, garlic, lemon grass, chilli and coriander. Mix well, then season to taste and stir in the egg.

Use your hands to shape the mixture into 4 large balls, then press them firmly into burger shapes. Place under a preheated hot grill and cook for 5 minutes on each side, or until golden and cooked through. Serve in warmed wholemeal buns with kale crisps on the side.

THAI BEEF & MIXED PEPPER STIR-FRY

A fragrant, nourishing meal to banish anxiety, depression and fatigue and encourage restful sleep.

Preparation time: 15 minutes
Cooking time: 10 minutes
Serves 4

1 tbsp **sesame oil**
1 **garlic clove**, finely chopped
500 g (1 lb) **lean beef fillet**,
 thinly sliced across the grain
1 **lemon grass stalk**, outer leaves
 removed and core finely chopped
2.5 cm (1 inch) piece of fresh **root ginger**,
 peeled and finely chopped
1 **red pepper**, cored, deseeded
 and thickly sliced
1 **green pepper**, cored,
 deseeded and thickly sliced
1 **onion**, thickly sliced
1 **red chilli**, deseeded and finely chopped
finely grated rind and juice of 2 **limes**
handful of fresh **coriander**, chopped, plus
 few sprigs, to garnish
sea salt and **black pepper**
rice or **noodles** to serve

Heat the oil in a wok or large frying pan over a high heat, add the garlic and beef and stir-fry for 2–3 minutes until lightly coloured.

Stir in the lemon grass and ginger and remove the pan from the heat. Remove the beef from the pan and set aside.

Add the peppers, onion and chilli to the pan and stir-fry for 2–3 minutes until the onions are just turning golden brown and are slightly softened.

Return the beef to the pan, stir in the lime rind and juice and the coriander, and season to taste. Serve in bowls with rice or noodles, garished with a sprig of coriander.

HERBY ARTICHOKE CASSEROLE

Don't hesitate to add whatever root vegetables you have to hand to this delicious casserole.

Preparation time: 15 minutes
Cooking time: 30 minutes
Serves 4
················

2 tbsps **olive oil**
1 large **onion**, chopped
2 **celery sticks**, chopped
3 **carrots**, chopped
2 **parsnips**, chopped
1 **fennel bulb**, outer leaves
    removed, chopped
1 **sweet potato**, peeled and chopped
2 tbsps **dried oregano**
1 tbsp **dried rosemary**
1 tsp **dried thyme**
½ tsp **dried marjoram**
½ tsp **dried basil**
600 ml (1 pint) **vegetable stock**
400 g (13 oz) can **butter beans**,
    rinsed and drained
400 g (13 oz) can **chickpeas**,
    rinsed and drained
200 g (7 oz) jar **artichoke hearts**, drained
sea salt and **black pepper**
couscous or **bulgar wheat**, to serve
    (optional)

Heat the oil in a large saucepan over a medium heat, add the onions, celery, carrots, parsnips, fennel and sweet potato and cook for about 5 minutes, or until the onions begin to soften.
·······································

Stir in the dried herbs and continue to cook for a further 5 minutes. Add the stock and bring to the boil, reduce the heat and simmer for 15 minutes, stirring frequently, until the vegetables are tender.
·······································

Add the butter beans, chickpeas and artichokes and continue to simmer for a further 5 minutes. Season to taste and serve immediately with couscous or bulgar wheat, if desired.
·······································

PENNE WITH TOMATO, ARTICHOKE & OLIVE SAUCE

Wholemeal penne is combined with antioxidant-rich tomatoes, nourishing olives and hormone-balancing artichokes.

Preparation time: 15 minutes
Cooking time: 25 minutes
Serves 4
....

1 tbsp **olive oil**
1 **onion**, finely chopped
2 **garlic cloves**, finely chopped
50 ml (2 fl oz) **red wine**
2 x 400 g (13 oz) cans **chopped tomatoes**
pinch of **sugar**
finely grated rind of ½ **lemon**
1 tsp **dried oregano**
75 g (3 oz) pitted **black olives**,
   roughly chopped
400 g (13 oz) **wholemeal penne**
small bunch of **basil**, torn
400 g (13 oz) can **artichoke hearts**,
   rinsed, drained and chopped
sea salt and **black pepper**
green salad, to serve

Heat the olive oil in a large, heavy-based saucepan over a medium-low heat, add the onion and garlic and cook gently for 5–6 minutes until softened.
....

Stir in the wine, tomatoes, sugar, lemon rind, oregano and olives and bring to the boil. Reduce the heat and simmer gently for 12–15 minutes.
....

Meanwhile, cook the pasta in a large saucepan of lightly salted boiling water for 11 minutes until 'al dente', or according to the packet instructions.
....

Add the basil and artichokes to the pasta sauce and cook gently until heated through. Season to taste, toss with the pasta and serve with a green salad.
....

CREAMY ROASTED PEPPERS WITH MIXED GRAINS

Any grains work well in this supper dish, designed to banish anxiety and set you up for a good night's sleep.

Preparation time: 10 minutes
Cooking time: 25–30 minutes
Serves 4

4 long **red peppers**, halved
    lengthways and deseeded
25 g (1 oz) **walnut** pieces, chopped
500 g (1 lb) cooked **mixed grains**,
    such as bulgar wheat, quinoa,
    brown rice or spelt
2 tbsps **lemon juice**
2 tbsps **sun-dried tomato paste**
3 tbsps chopped **mixed herbs**, such as
    parsley, tarragon, chives and thyme
sea salt and **black pepper**

Cheese filling
350 g (11½ oz) **quark** or **cream cheese**
3 tbsps chopped **mixed herbs**, such as
    parsley, tarragon, chives and thyme
finely grated rind of ½ **lemon**
2 tbsps toasted **mixed seeds**

Mix together all the filling ingredients in a small bowl and season to taste. Arrange the peppers, cut side up, on a baking sheet and spoon in the filling. Scatter with the walnuts and place in a preheated oven, 200°C (400°F), Gas Mark 6, for 25–30 minutes until the peppers are tender and the filling is golden.

Meanwhile, warm the mixed grains in a large saucepan, add the lemon juice, tomato paste and mixed herbs and season to taste.

Spoon the grains on to serving plates, arrange the stuffed peppers on top and serve immediately.

SQUASH, CHICKPEA & SWEET POTATO TAGINE

Rich in antioxidants, fibre and nerve-boosting B vitamins, this vegetable-packed, fragrant tagine is perfect for chilly nights.

Preparation time: 25 minutes
Cooking time: about 40 minutes
Serves 4–6
....

2 tbsps **olive oil**
2 **onions**, chopped
2 tsps **ground coriander**
2 tsps **ground cinnamon**
2 tsps **ground cumin**
1 tsp **chilli powder**
1 cm (½ in) piece of fresh **root ginger**, peeled and grated
3 **garlic cloves**, unpeeled, crushed
1 tbsp **concentrated tomato purée**
1 large **butternut squash**, peeled, deseeded and cut into chunks
2 **sweet potatoes**, peeled and cut into chunks
2 **carrots**, cut into chunks
2 **parsnips**, cut into chunks
50 g (2 oz) soft **dried apricots**, chopped
750 ml (1¼ pints) **vegetable stock**
finely grated rind and juice of 1 **lemon**
400 g (13 oz) can **chickpeas**, rinsed and drained
3 tbsps chopped **coriander**
sea salt and **black pepper**
pomegranate seeds, to garnish
bulgar wheat, to serve

Heat the oil in a large saucepan over a medium heat, add the onions and cook gently for about 10 minutes until soft. Stir in the coriander, cinnamon, cumin, chilli powder, ginger and garlic, then the tomato purée.

....

Cook for a further 2–3 minutes, then add the squash, sweet potatoes, carrots, parsnips and apricots and stir well. Add the stock, lemon rind and juice, bring to the boil, then reduce the heat and simmer, uncovered, until the vegetables are almost cooked.

....

Add the chickpeas and the fresh coriander, then season to taste. Cook for a further 10–15 minutes, then remove from the heat. Serve immediately with bulgar wheat, sprinkled with pomegranate seeds.

....

WATERMELON, GINGER & LIME GRANITA

This fresh, light dessert is the ideal way to round off a meal, encouraging restful sleep and easing irritability.

Preparation time: 15 minutes, plus cooling and freezing
Cooking time: 10 minutes
Serves 4

....

125 ml (4 fl oz) **lime juice**
875 g (1 ¾ lb) **watermelon**, peeled and deseeded
finely grated rind of 2 **limes**
125 g (4 oz) **demerara sugar**
5 cm (2 in) piece of fresh **root ginger**, peeled and finely grated
mint sprigs, to decorate

Place the lime juice, watermelon and half the lime rind in a blender or food processor and blend until smooth. Strain to remove any bits of seed.

....

Transfer 125 ml (4 fl oz) of the mixture to a small saucepan, stir in the sugar, the remaining lime rind and half the ginger and place over a medium heat until the sugar has dissolved. Remove from the heat and allow to cool.

....

Stir the cooled syrup into the watermelon purée with the remaining ginger. Pour into a shallow container and freeze for 2 hours, beating with a fork every 20 minutes or so to break up the ice crystals, until it has a thick, slushy consistency. Serve in glass dishes decorated with mint sprigs.

....

BRAZIL NUT & BANANA PARFAIT

Rich in protein, the oats and nuts in this sweet, crunchy dessert will help keep blood sugar levels stable.

Preparation time: 15 minutes
Cooking time: 15 minutes
Serves 4

100 g (3½ oz) **brazil nuts**, chopped
125 ml (4 fl oz) **maple syrup**
50 g (2 oz) **porridge oats**
400 ml (14 fl oz) **live Greek yogurt**
1 tsp **vanilla extract**
1 tsp **ground cinnamon**
2 tbsps **icing sugar**
4 ripe but firm **bananas**, sliced
2 tsps **lemon juice**
2 tsps **demerara sugar**

Place the brazil nuts and maple syrup in a small saucepan over a low heat and cook until the syrup bubbles. Remove from the heat and stir in the oats. Tip out on to a nonstick baking sheet and place in a preheated oven, 160°C (325°F), Gas Mark 3, for 10 minutes, or until the oats are toasted and sticky.

Mix the yogurt with the vanilla, cinnamon and icing sugar and set aside. Reserve 4 slices of banana for decoration, then place the remaining bananas in another bowl with the lemon juice and demerara sugar and toss to coat.

Divide half the yogurt mixture between 4 glass bowls or sundae glasses, top with half the bananas, then half the nut mixture. Repeat the layers, finishing with the nut mixture. Decorate with the reserved banana slices and chill until ready to serve.

ICED BERRIES WITH DARK CHOCOLATE SAUCE

This is possibly the easiest dessert you can make, rich in antioxidants for health and chocolate to raise your spirits.

Preparation time: 5 minutes
Cooking time: 5 minutes
Serves 4
....

125 g (4 oz) **plain dark chocolate**
125 ml (4 fl oz) **live natural yogurt**
2 tbsps **icing sugar**, plus extra for dusting
500 g (1 lb) mixed **frozen berries**
  (raspberries, strawberries, blueberries,
  currants or blackberries)

Melt the chocolate in a heatproof bowl set over a saucepan of gently simmering water, making sure the water does not touch the bottom of the bowl.
....

Stir in the yogurt and icing sugar and mix until smooth. Scatter the frozen berries on 4 serving plates.
....

While the chocolate is still hot, pour the sauce over the frozen berries and dust with a little icing sugar. Serve immediately.
....

BAKED FIGS WITH MASCARPONE

This is an elegant dessert rich in fibre and calcium. The zesty ginger works both to warm and to aid digestion.

Preparation time: 10 minutes
Cooking time: 15-20 minutes
Serves 4
....

8-12 ripe **figs**, halved
1 tbsp **butter**, cut into small chunks
2 tbsps **wild honey**
1 tbsp dark soft **brown sugar**
1 tsb **ground allspice**
2 tsps **ground cinnamon**
finely grated rind and juice of 1 **orange**
125 g (4 oz) **mascarpone cheese**
1 cm (½ in) piece of fresh **root ginger**,
   peeled and roughly chopped
½ tsp **vanilla extract**
2 tbsps **icing sugar**

Arrange the figs in an ovenproof dish, cut-side up, and dot with butter. Stir together the honey, sugar, allspice, cinnamon, orange juice and half the orange rind in a small bowl, and drizzle over the figs. Bake in a preheated oven, 200°C (400°F), Gas Mark 6, for 15-20 minutes until bubbling.

....

Meanwhile, place the mascarpone, ginger, vanilla, icing sugar and the remaining orange rind in a blender or food processor and blend until smooth and fluffy.

....

Place the figs on serving plates, top each with a spoonful of mascarpone and drizzle with the fig juices. Serve warm or cold.

....

DARK CHOCOLATE & RASPBERRY SOUFFLÉ

Don't feel guilty about indulging in this delicious dessert: it will help you relax and lift your mood.

Preparation time: 10 minutes
Cooking time: 20 minutes
Serves 4
....

100 g (3½ oz) **plain dark chocolate**
3 **eggs**, separated
50 g (2 oz) **self-raising flour**, sifted
40 g (1½ oz) **caster sugar**
150 g (5 oz) **raspberries**,
   plus extra to serve (optional)
Icing sugar for dusting

Melt the chocolate in a heatproof bowl set over a saucepan of gently simmering water, making sure the water does not touch the bottom of the bowl. Allow to cool a little, then beat in the egg yolks and fold in the flour.
....

Whisk the egg whites and caster sugar in a clean bowl, using a hand-held electric whisk, until they form soft peaks. Beat a spoonful of the egg whites into the chocolate mixture to loosen it, then gently fold in the rest.
....

Divide the raspberries between 4 lightly greased ramekins, pour over the chocolate mixture, then place in a preheated oven, 190°C (375°F), Gas Mark 5, for 12–15 minutes until the soufflés have risen.
....

Dust with icing sugar and serve immediately with extra raspberries, if liked.
....

TIPSY BLUEBERRY & MASCARPONE POTS

Although alcohol isn't recommended in most mood-lifting menus, a little can lift your spirits and help you relax.

Preparation time: 15 minutes, plus soaking
Serves 4
....

200 g (7 oz) **blueberries**
2 tbsps **kirsch** or **vodka**
150 g (5 oz) **mascarpone cheese**
150 ml (5 fl oz) **live natural yogurt**
2 tbsps **icing sugar**
finely grated rind and juice of 1 **lime**

Place the blueberries in a bowl, drizzle with the alcohol and leave to soak for at least 1 hour.
....

Set aside a quarter of the blueberries in alchohol in a separate bowl and roughly mash the remaining soaked blueberries with a fork.
....

Beat together the mascarpone and yogurt until smooth, then stir in the icing sugar and the lime rind and juice.
....

Divide the mashed blueberries between 4 glass serving dishes and top with the mascarpone mixture. Sprinkle the whole blueberries on top and chill until ready to serve.
....

CHERRY & NECTARINE PAVLOVA

Use nectarines or peaches in this healthy pavlova. If you like things a little creamier, use crème fraîche instead of fromage frais.

Preparation time: 20 minutes, plus cooling
Cooking time: 1 hour
Serves 4
....

3 **egg whites**
175 g (6 oz) **caster sugar**
1 tsp strong black **coffee**
1 tsp **vanilla extract**
250 g (8 oz) **fromage frais**
125 g (4 oz) **cherries**
125 g (4 oz) **nectarines**, stoned and sliced

Whisk the egg whites in a large bowl with a hand-held electric whisk until stiff peaks form. Fold in 1 tbsp of the sugar, then gradually whisk in the remainder until smooth, glossy and very stiff. Fold in the black coffee and vanilla.
....

Spoon the meringue on to a baking sheet lined with nonstick baking paper and spread out to form a 20 cm (8 inch) diameter round. Make a slight hollow in the centre of the meringue and place in a preheated oven, 120°C (250°F), Gas Mark ½, for 1 hour until the meringue is crisp. Leave to cool.
....

Peel the paper off the back of the meringue and place the meringue on a serving plate. Fill the hollow with the fromage frais and arrange the cherries and nectarine pieces on top. Serve immediately.
....

FIG & GRAPE TARTS

These crunchy tarts are simple to make and contain enough fruit to give you an antioxidant and fibre boost.

Preparation time: 20 minutes, plus cooling
Cooking time: 4 minutes
Makes 12
....

300 g (10 oz) **filo pastry**
75 g (3 oz) **butter**, melted,
   plus extra for greasing
3 tbsps seedless **raspberry jam**
425 ml (14½ fl oz) **live Greek yogurt**
2 tbsps **wild honey**
1 tsp **vanilla extract**
pinch of **sea salt**
25 g (1 oz) **ground almonds**
handful of **redcurrants**
handful of seedless **black grapes**, halved
seeds and pulp from 2 **passion fruit**
4 ripe **figs**, quartered
handful of **raspberries**
2 tbsps **apricot jam**, warmed

Brush the filo pastry sheets, one at a time, with melted butter, then stack them up in a neat pile. Cut the pile into 4–6 squares, depending on their size.
....

Use the individual pastry squares to line a greased 12-hole muffin tin, placing them one on top of the other to line the holes. Offset the pastry squares in each hole to create an uneven, ruched edge.
....

Place in a preheated oven, 180°C (350°F), Gas Mark 4, for 4 minutes or until the pastry is golden and crisp. Remove from the oven and allow to cool in the tin for 10 minutes, then transfer the pastry cases to a wire rack to cool completely.
....

Place the pastry cases on a serving plate and divide the raspberry jam between them. Mix the yogurt with the honey, vanilla, salt and ground almonds in a small bowl and spoon the mixture on top of the jam.
....

Arrange the currants, grapes, passion fruit, figs and raspberries in the cases, then brush the tops of the tarts with the warmed apricot jam. Serve immediately.
....

TROPICAL FRUIT SALAD WITH GREEN TEA SYRUP

Brimming with antioxidants to ease stress, encourage sleep and aid digestion, this fruit salad makes a nice breakfast, too!

Preparation time: 20 minutes, plus infusing and chilling
Cooking time: 7 minutes
Serves 6

2 large **mangoes**, peeled, stoned and diced
2 large **papaya**, peeled, deseeded and diced
1 small **pineapple**, peeled, cored and diced
2 **kiwi fruit**, peeled and sliced
400 g (13 oz) can **lychees**, drained
250 g (8 oz) **green grapes**

Syrup
125 g (4 oz) **caster sugar**
300 ml (½ pint) **water**
grated rind and juice of 1 **lime**
2.5 cm (1 inch) piece of fresh **root ginger**, peeled and chopped
1 **green teabag**

To make the syrup, place the sugar, measurement water, lime rind and juice and ginger in a saucepan over a gentle heat and cook, stirring occasionally, until the sugar has dissolved. Bring to the boil and simmer for 5 minutes.

Remove from the heat and add the teabag, then leave to infuse for 10 minutes. Remove the teabag and pour the syrup into a jug. Chill for 10 minutes.

Place all the prepared fruit in a large bowl and strain the cooled syrup over the top. Chill until ready to serve.

ORANGE, GINGER & SESAME RICE PUDDING

This is a tasty treat, combining warming ginger with brown rice to balance mood and blood sugar.

Preparation time: 10 minutes
Cooking time: 1¾ hours
Serves 4
....

325 ml (11 fl oz) **double cream**
   or **soya cream**
300 ml (10 fl oz) **water**
100 g (3½ oz) **brown rice**
2 **oranges**
2.5 cm (1 in) piece of fresh **root ginger**,
   peeled and grated
3 **egg yolks**
3 tbsps **demerara sugar**
1 tsp **ground cinnamon**
2 tsps **vanilla extract**
1 tsp **butter**, melted
3 tbsps toasted **sesame seeds**

Place the cream, measurement water and rice in a large, heavy-based saucepan and add the juice and finely grated rind of 1 orange. Peel and chop the remaining orange and add to the pan with the ginger.
....

Place the saucepan over a medium heat, cover and bring to the boil. Reduce the heat and simmer gently, stirring regularly, for about 1½ hours until the rice is soft and all of the liquid has been absorbed, adding a little water if it dries out too quickly.
....

Place the egg yolks in a bowl with the sugar, cinnamon, vanilla and butter and stir to combine. Add to the pan and cook over a low heat, stirring constantly, for 5–10 minutes until the mixture thickens. Remove from the heat and sprinkle with the sesame seeds. Serve warm or cold.
....

CHOCOLATE-DIPPED FRUIT

Chocolate satisfies cravings and, combined with fruit, offers a nutritious snack with maximum feel-good factor.

Preparation time: 10 minutes, plus chilling
Cooking time: 5–10 minutes
Serves 4

75 g (3 oz) **white chocolate**
75 g (3 oz) **plain dark chocolate**
400 g (13 oz) **strawberries** with stalks
125 g (4 oz) **cherries** with stalks
125 g (4 oz) **Cape gooseberries**

Melt the chocolates in 2 separate heat-proof bowls set over saucepans of gently simmering water, taking care not to let the water touch the bottoms of the bowls. Allow to cool slightly.

Half-dip half the fruit in the dark chocolate, allowing the excess to drip back into the bowl. Transfer to a baking sheet lined with nonstick baking paper to set.

Repeat with the remaining fruit and the white chocolate. Chill in the refrigerator for at least 10–15 minutes, or until ready to eat.

POACHED APRICOTS WITH ORANGE FLOWER WATER

The pistachios in this light, fragrant dessert are rich in omega oils and energy-boosting B vitamins.

Preparation time: 10 minutes, plus cooling
Cooking time: 5 minutes
Serves 4
....

400 g (13 oz) soft **dried apricots**
350 ml (12 fl oz) **apple and elderflower juice**
2 tbsps **orange flower water**
½ tsp **ground cinnamon**
2 tbsps **clear honey**
75 g (3 oz) shelled unsalted **pistachios**, crushed
live natural yogurt or **vanilla ice cream**, to serve

Place the apricots, apple and elderflower juice, orange flower water, cinnamon and honey in a heavy-based saucepan over a medium-high heat and bring to the boil. Reduce the heat and simmer for 2–3 minutes until the apricots are plump.
....

Transfer to a large serving bowl and set aside to cool slightly. Scatter with the pistachios and serve warm or cold, with yogurt or ice cream.
....

RESOURCES

Action on Addiction
Tel: 0300 330 0659
Email: action@actiononaddiction.org.uk
Website: www.actiononaddiction.org.uk

Anxiety UK
Tel: 0161 227 9898
Email: info@anxietyuk.org.uk
Website: www.anxietyuk.org.uk

Bipolar UK
Tel: 020 7931 6480
Email: info@bipolaruk.org.uk
Website: www.bipolaruk.org.uk

**British Association for Counselling
and Psychotherapy**
Tel: 0870 443 5252
Email: bacp@bacp.co.uk
Website: www.bacp.co.uk

British Meditation Society
Tel: 01460 62921
Website: http://www.britishmeditationsociety.org

British Nutrition Foundation
Tel: 020 7557 7930
Email: postbox@nutrition.org.uk
Website: www.nutrition.org.uk

British Wheel of Yoga
Tel: 01529 306 851
Website: www.bwy.org.uk

Depression Alliance
Tel: 0845 1232320
Email: information@depressionalliance.org
Website: www.depressionalliance.org

Depression UK
Email: info@depressionuk.org
Website: www.depressionuk.org

MIND
Tel: 0845 766 1063
Email: contact@mind.org.uk
Website: www.mind.org.uk

The Nutrition Society
Tel: 020 7602 0228
Email: office@nutsoc.org.uk
Website: www.nutsoc.org.uk

National Association for Pre-menstrual Syndrome
Tel: 0844 8157311
Email: contact@pms.org.uk
Website: www.pms.org.uk

PNI.org.uk (Post Natal Illness)
Email: enquiries@pni.org.uk
Website: www.pni.org.uk

The Seasonal Affective Disorder Association
Email: contact@sada.org.uk
Website: www.sada.org.uk

Samaritans
Helpline: 08457 909090
Email: jo@samaritans.org
Website: www.samaritans.org.uk

Sane
Helpline: 0845 767 8000
Email: info@sane.org.uk
Website: www.sane.org.uk

INDEX

Acknowledgements

Gill Paul would like to thank the very talented team at Octopus: Denise Bates, who came up with the idea for the series; Jo Wilson, Katy Denny and Alex Stetter who edited the books so efficiently and made it all work; and to the design team of Jonathan Christie and Isabel de Cordova for making it all look so gorgeous. Thank you also to Karel Bata for all the support and for eating my cooking.

Karen Sullivan would like to thank Cole, Luke and Marcus.

Picture Credits

Commissioned photography © Octopus Publishing Group/Will Heap apart from the following:

Getty Images
Anthony Lee 10.

Octopus Publishing Group
David Munns 87; Lis Parsons 41, 49, 61, 75, 77, 89, 93, 115; William Shaw 65, 67, 71, 101, 117, 119.

Thinkstock
Hemera 16; iStockphoto 5, 7, 8, 9, 12, 18, 21, 22, 27, 34.